preaching
to the
contemporary mind

preaching
to the
contemporary mind

merrill r. abbey

ABINGDON PRESS   NEW YORK • NASHVILLE

PREACHING TO THE CONTEMPORARY MIND

Copyright © 1963 by Abingdon Press

Library of Congress Catalog Card Number: 63-7763

to my children

mary
richard
stuart
nancy

preface

Although this book addresses itself specifically to the work of preaching, it speaks to all who are in earnest about Christian witness that reaches the life of this time: teachers of adults, counselors of youth, those concerned about Christian communication through the vast possibilities of the mass media, all who work with the outreach of the gospel.

The needs of preachers, however, have been the constant concern of this study—though this is not another book of homiletic principles. There is little here about how to organize sermons, how to illustrate, how to deliver the message. At the end of each chapter, to be sure, there are suggestions for further study, including practical exercises by which the reader can put this material to work. But these are designed to develop skill in relation to homiletic principles the student has already learned in the excellent books now available, not to travel with him over this beginning ground.

Pastoral and preaching demands through nearly two decades of dialogue with the college and university mind and an interlude in the bustling downtown of a major city have kept me struggling to find ways of interpreting the gospel to the fast-moving mind of this time. During all this period two questions have been uppermost: How can I get inside these complex minds? How can the vital heart of the Christian message be conveyed to them where they are? The endeavor to bring together the answers to these two questions has been

7

the baffling, fascinating, often exciting preoccupation of the years.

In a subsequent and briefer period the adventure has been transferred to the theological seminary classroom. The same central questions have focused the attention of students in an advanced course, "Preaching to the Contemporary Mind." The chapters which follow have grown out of this cumulative experience.

I am indebted to many teachers. Acknowledgments of identifiable borrowings from published sources have been carefully made in reference notes. No footnoting can cover my obligation to Dr. Horace Greeley Smith, Emeritus President of Garrett Theological Seminary, who, as my teacher of preaching long ago, deepened my love of the calling, gave me confidence that I could grow in it, and pointed me in directions that have proven increasingly profitable through the years. Dr. John Capps Irwin, James E. MacMurray Professor of Preaching and Dean of the Faculty of Garrett, has given invaluable aid, guiding my orientation from pastorate to professorship, encouraging the development of this project, sharing wise counsel on many a preaching problem, and doing me the honor or reading and criticizing the manuscript. An earlier version of Chapter Two first appeared in *The Garrett Tower*, and I am indebted to the editor, Professor Henry E. Kolbe, for helpful consultation concerning it and for permission to reissue it in its present form. Last, and most constantly, I am grateful to my wife, who has given valuable assistance by making the index, and whose enthusiastic support, having sustained my ministry from the beginning, has made this book possible and filled the work with joy.

MERRILL R. ABBEY

contents

part one—the mind in today's world

9

part two—the gospel and today's mind

part one ──────────
the mind in today's world

1
achieving a meeting of minds

To interpret the gospel in the latter half of this century is to communicate in Babel. There ambitious builders gloried in a new technology: "they had brick for stone, and bitumen for mortar" (Gen. 11:3). If the innovation did not release the power of the atom or probe the limits of space, it did open vistas of opportunity formerly undreamed. Pride came hard on the heels of accomplishment. To be sure, they did not boast, as did an East Berlin newspaper concerning Sputnik: "The eighth day of creation, which has given the earth its second moon, is a reality . . . With such the Bible cannot compete." [1] Their guiding motive, however, was gathered up in the proposal, "Let us make a name for ourselves." Like contemporary pride, theirs had its taproot in anxiety. Estranged in the world, and fearing to be alone, they proposed their proud project protectively—"lest we be scattered abroad upon the face of the whole earth." The outcome sounds sadly familiar: "So the Lord scattered them abroad from there over the face of all the earth, and they left off building the city" (Gen. 11:8).

To interpret the gospel today is to speak to people thus scattered. As the universe grows larger, the divisions of earth run deeper. Symbolic is the first adventurer in the exploration of space. When Yuri Gegarin stepped into his cosmic capsule, his feet had never touched any but Russian soil. When, minutes later, he emerged as the first man to have ventured far in space and orbited the earth, he still knew only Russian soil. In an age of cosmic thrust and parochial insight, our scat-

[1] Quoted in Richard W. Solberg, *God and Caesar in East Germany* (New York: The Macmillan Company, 1961), p. 242. Used by permission.

tering prompts concern. In crucial need of a reconciling message, we are the age of propaganda's burnt children who have learned to ask concerning any communication, "Who speaks through its author?" and concerning every publication, "What powers—economic, political, ideological—shape its policy?" We look for the ventriloquist back of every speaker in an age when "interests have taken the place of truth." [2] Can those who speak the Christian message hope to escape this probing skepticism?

Words themselves no longer pass as common coin. In days when wanderers from the West could cross freely into the eastern sector of Berlin, signs at the entrance points proclaimed, "You are now entering Democratic Berlin." Returning from the Communist domain to the democratic West, one read, "You are now leaving Democratic Berlin." In 1961, the Secretary of State found it useful to offer a "glossary of Soviet definitions"—such words as "peace," "aggression," "People's Democracy," "self-determination," "negotiations," "agreement," "assurances," "lawlessness," and "neutrality" defined in ways which reverse previous understandings of the same terms in the part of the world we have known.[3]

Not alone in the political arena have the key words been thus polarized. The minister of the "Lutheran Hour" has described the perplexity of an immigrant standing before a newsstand attempting to grasp the English usage of one of Christianity's basic words: love. He finds it on a magazine illustrated with pictures of scantily clad girls; but just when he has this meaning associated with the word, he finds it on a magazine whose cover displays a happy family relaxing in a pleasant home. Before he has reconciled these diverse meanings, he is startled to come upon a religious magazine displaying a man on a cross, with the caption, "God's love

[2] Cf. Helmut Thielicke, *Nihilism* (New York: Harper & Row, Publishers, 1961), p. 24.

[3] *Chicago Daily News*, July 11, 1961.

for sinners." [4] Scarcely one of the cardinal words of the New Testament vocabulary has escaped such shattering of its original intent. No man can effectively proclaim the gospel now unless he devotes constant study to the meanings and attitudes already established in the minds he must address. Only so can he foresee what meaning they will derive from the words and symbols he employs.

This need not startle the twentieth century interpreter. It has been the problem of those who proclaimed the gospel from its earliest times. Back of the familiar text, "In the beginning was the Word" (John 1:1), and the noble hymn which sings its way through the ensuing verses, lies the complex Hebrew theology of the Word, which had met the even more involved Greek philosophy of the Logos to form the pattern of assumptions in the minds to which the Fourth Gospel brought the message of the Incarnation. No reader can grasp the meaning of the Letter to the Hebrews unless he understands something of the Judaic doctrines and practices associated with atonement; for these were the presuppositions in the minds of the intended readers—these and the then current Platonic philosophy which also underlies this epistle. No one now reads the First Letter of John intelligently apart from a background understanding of Gnosticism, since it was the docetic doctrines of that movement which occupied the minds to which this epistle was addressed. From the first Christian generation until now, it has been the task of preachers and teachers to understand the minds they must currently reach and to find words and symbols adequate to convey the gospel meaning to them.

How can the messenger accomplish this task in the baffling decades remaining in this century? What is the nature of the mind to which he must speak? What issues are crucial? How can a message undilutedly Christian meet the moving target

[4] Oswald C. J. Hoffman, *Life Crucified* (Grand Rapids: Wm. B. Eerdmans Publishing Co., 1959), p. 30.

of that changing mind with accuracy? To these questions this book addresses its quest.

II

The need to achieve a meeting of minds inheres in the nature of preaching as of all significant discourse. A statesman of the last century spoke of oratory as "animated conversation," and a creative preacher subsequently borrowed the term to describe the sermon. Thus to stress the conversational is not to commend the offhand and informal, but to recognize that minds change only as they are engaged in the active give and take of dialogue. The passive listener learns little and his attitudes change less. The growing science of communication makes it clear that overcoming passivity is a primary requisite of the purposeful speaker. A considerable volume of experimental data sustains the conclusions that learning is facilitated by verbalization on the part of the learner, that more changes of opinion occur in discussion than in passive listening, and that attitude changes are greatly advanced when the subject is involved in role playing.[5] This verifies the conviction of effective preachers, that the listener's mind must be engaged in an active project in co-operative thinking. The speaker raises questions which require answer; anticipates the listener's objections, putting them more cogently than he himself could; and states the case not as an ultimatum handed down but as an insight at which speaker and listener arrive together.

Such preaching has sometimes been characterized as group counseling. The term has limitations. A congregation is not a counseling group, and the listener in the pew is not a counselee in the exchange of the intimate circle. Yet the counseling concept suggests much. Preaching can be so handled as not only to elicit the active participation of the listener, but to help him feel that he is understood and accepted—that, no

[5] Carl I. Hovland, Irving L. Janis, and Harold H. Kelley, *Communication and Persuasion* (New Haven: Yale University Press, 1953), pp. 215-237.

longer alone with his struggles, he shares them with the man who speaks and with many of those who listen with him.

Both in counseling and in preaching influence rests on empathy, sometimes defined as a deep

state of identification of personalities in which one person so feels himself into the other as temporarily to lose his own identity. It is in this profound and somewhat mysterious process of empathy that understanding, influence, and the other significant relations between persons take place. Thus in discussing empathy we are considering not only the key process in counseling, but the key likewise to practically all the work of preachers, teachers, and others whose vocation depends upon the influencing of people.[6]

This identification is the more essential to the preaching situation because the listener can make no verbal answer. As Edgar N. Jackson points out, under conditions in which they cannot talk back, persons have a special need of an atmosphere in which they can "feel back." [7] Without an open channel of understanding the preacher is defeated by the listener's hostility or his lapse into apathy.

This insight from contemporary psychology finds confirmation in the great moments of the Bible. The familiar words of Isaiah are typical:

> Come now, let us reason together,
>   says the Lord:
> though your sins are like scarlet,
>   they shall be as white as snow;
> though they are red like crimson,
>   they shall become like wool.

[6] Rollo May, *The Art of Counseling* (Nashville: Abingdon Press, 1936), p. 75.

[7] Edgar N. Jackson, A *Psychology for Preaching* (Manhasset, New York: Channel Press, Inc., 1961), p. 64.

If you are willing and obedient,
    you shall eat the good of the land;
But if you refuse and rebel,
    you shall be devoured by the sword;
    for the mouth of the Lord has spoken.
                                    —Isa. 1:18-20

Here the prophetic preacher is precipitating an encounter between God and his people. His summons to them to "reason together" resembles Job's plea for an opportunity to lay his case before God in the give and take of protest and response— "There an upright man could reason with him" (Job 23:7). Isaiah speaks thus of the encounter with God as a "reasoning" exchange in which the people's false assumptions are challenged. They have been content to suppose forgiveness cheap and easy, thinking unconditionally that "though your sins are like scarlet, they shall be as white as snow." But the prophet will accept no Voltairean "God will forgive; that's what he's there for." His message offers pardon conditioned on confession and obedience. Before the people can respond, however, their errors must be corrected in a dialogic exchange: "let us reason together."

In Chapter Two, as we examine the theological link between authority and communication, we shall pursue this matter further. For the present it is important to note that the quest for a meeting of minds is vital if preaching is to fulfill its function as the spoken word by which men are precipitated into a state of "ultimate concern" in a real encounter with God.

III

Such encounter is achieved only by the preacher who is first a listener. A suspicion has long been abroad that preachers listen to the wrong voices. In 1918 Eugene V. Debs cynically predicted, "When Wall Street yells war, you may rest assured every pulpit in the land will yell war." Nearly a generation

18

earlier, Robert Ingersoll had declared that every pulpit is occupied by "an intellectual slave," who "dare not preach his honest thought." Too often justified by ministerial failure, these accusations should not be allowed to obscure the necessity that the interpreter of the gospel *be a listener*, not only to the voice of God heard in prayer and the study of the Word, but to the questions and assumptions of the people.

A time-tested advice urges the young minister to preach mainly on the great themes of the faith. It is wise counsel. No search for current ideas or novel texts can so feed a rewarding interpretation of the gospel as does a steady exposure to such centralities as God's creative sovereignty; his righteous judgment; his redeeming love; his incarnation in Christ; his reconciling act in Jesus' life, death, and resurrection; his forgiveness; his justifying grace; his gift of life new and eternal; his call to the Kingdom; his final victory. But who can preach with compelling power until he learns to relate the great themes of the faith to the central questions men ask? A generation ago, one of the wisest leaders of the church declared that at the beginning of his ministry he had looked ahead with searching study to determine as nearly as he could what would be the pivotal issues of the next twenty-five years. He resolved, he said, to address his message to these convinced that there could be no significant ministry oriented to peripheral issues. Most of us would fear to lay claim to prophetic insight that can foresee the major issues of a quarter century; every minister, however, can learn to identify the crucial issues of his own time and to address the cardinal affirmations of the gospel to the burning questions men are struggling to decide.

In Chapters Three and Four we shall deal in some detail with this search for the central. It is enough here to note that "listening" to the minds and hearts of men is an important aspect of the preacher's reading. Let him read history and philosophy not only to learn the events and the conclusions at which thinkers arrived, but to find his way more fully into the questions men have persistently asked across the generations, with awakened imagination, and understanding heart, deeper comprehension of the appeal or challenge they offer to the Christian faith. Let him read the thinkers of his own time not alone for what they say that can reinforce his message, but to understand the problems with which they grapple, the difficulties they see, and—where they take issue with the faith as he knows it—the deep reasons for their divergence. Let him expose himself to the mass media not merely to follow their ever-changing image of his time, but to understand, if he can, what they take for granted and what that tells him about the unspoken assumptions of the mass audience they attract.

Against the background insights thus gained, the parish minister who is lovingly attentive can etch a more personal and intimate knowledge of the minds of men from his daily pastoral ministrations. On the staff of a large metropolitan church, a young assistant minister busy with doctoral studies in the allied fields of social work and education proved surprisingly creative. Under his guidance apathetic groups came alive, programs found vitality, individuals discovered their potentialities and achieved in ways they had not thought possible. Often his colleagues found him in his office after a long day carefully setting down notes about the meeting he had just completed. He was never through when the people went home and the lights in the meeting room had been turned off. Instead he went to his desk and carefully wrote out who had been present, what the activities had been, the responses of named individuals to successive steps in the procedures, the needs of which he had become aware, the problems he saw emerging, some indication of what the next steps should be. He worked with groups with a sensitive awareness of individual persons kept current by this daily discipline.

Just so, effective preachers do not speak to a faceless collection of people called a congregation. Their message keeps its quality of encounter because they address it to persons with a clear and currrent understanding of the questions individuals are asking, the issues with which they wrestle, the temptations that assail them, the pains they bear. Methods vary. One minister with a large staff refuses to permit the load of counseling to be lifted from his shoulders, sure that he cannot preach unless he is thus in touch with the struggles of individuals. Another refuses to surrender to an assistant the everlasting round of calls on the sick and troubled. Others go weekly to the empty sanctuary and sit in the pews of many of their people, trying the while to enter more sensitively into their concerns. Some use the church membership roll as a daily prayer list by which they are reminded of the needs and struggles of those for whom they intercede. One takes a long weekly walk through the darkened streets of his parish, rethinking his sermon trying to see how its message will sound to the individuals whose homes he passes, and how he can best touch them in their personal centers of concern.

Consider the discipline by which one veteran minister keeps his message personal. At the beginning of his weekly sermon preparation he sets down on paper the initials of a dozen or more persons with whom he has had pastoral contact in the preceding seven days. In each case he puts opposite the initials a sentence summary of a situation or need of which he has become aware: a grief, a lonely struggle, a besetting temptation, a twisted attitude, an unsolved problem. With the list before him, he says to himself: "This is a cross section of next Sunday's congregation. Any truth of the gospel that finds a mark must do so in the midst of such tensions, challenges, and anxieties as these. Unless this sermon can do business with these minds in these conditions, it will do no business." His sermons partake of the nature of animated conversation because from the beginning they are *developed* in conversation with persons with names, faces, and vividly felt needs.

IV

To achieve a meeting of minds the interpreter of the gospel needs not only his own analysis of the central issues and his constantly current awareness of the needs of individuals,

21

but some perceptive understanding of the underlying moods which run through the life of his generation. Five may be suggested as typical of our period.

First, and everywhere obvious, is a mood which seeks what might be called salvation by survey. From the teen-ager who cannot possibly know what to wear to the picnic until she has called half-a-dozen of her friends, to the Parent-Teacher Association determining how much time Junior *should* spend on his homework by means of a poll designed to discover how much time the "average pupil" *does* spend, to the businessman accepting kickbacks because "everybody does it," this mood which seeks guides to conduct by counting noses or studying the reactions of one's peers runs through our society. Its menace lies in the tendency of the "average pupil," on discovering that the less he does the less he is expected to do, to decrease his effort still further; or of the man who discovers that he is somewhat more chaste than the majority delineated in the Kinsey Reports to allow himself more liberties. Thus, as Joseph Wood Krutch observes, studies made a decade from now will show an average depressed still more. Society may be expected to require "less and less of its members who are pursuing the normal as it descends to lower and lower levels." [8]

A second mood is that of retreat from idealism. What Dorothy Parker satirized in her poem, "The Veteran," has become a widespread, debilitating malady of the mind and emotions.

> When I was young and bold and strong,
> Oh, right was right, and wrong was wrong!
> My plume on high, my flag unfurled,
> I rode away to right the world.
> "Come out, you dogs, and fight!" said I,
> And wept there was but once to die.

[8] *The Measure of Man* (New York: The Bobbs-Merrill Company, Inc., 1954), p. 224.

But I am old; and good and bad
Are woven in a crazy plaid.
I sit and say, "The world is so;
And he is wise who lets it go.
A battle lost, a battle won—
The difference is small, my son."

Inertia rides and riddles me;
The which is called Philosophy.[9]

Helmut Thielicke, writing out of the anguish of Europe, remarks that most people sixty years of age have changed their essential foundations in some "ism" about three times in their lives; and that the twenty year olds, observing this fact, have grown skeptical of all fixed beliefs convinced that "at the tail end of this parade of idols there is *Nothing*, a *Nothing* which is always dressed up in some new ideology, but still nothing but nothingness." [10] German representatives to the Amsterdam Assembly of the World Council of Churches set down this attitude as one of the "axioms" from which the common mind of their country tended to proceed. In their phrasing, it ran: "There is no sense in bothering about great causes, for every attempt to support such things is utterly useless, and you are just left holding the baby!" [11] In the timorousness which descended on public life in the wake of the McCarthy era, in the widespread turn of students from crusading to a search for security, and in the recoil of the church from the social gospel this mood is equally visible in America.

A third mood accepts as self-evident the dictum that "the end justifies the means." This is not only a cardinal principle

[9] From *Not So Deep as a Well* by Dorothy Parker. Copyright 1926, 1953 by Dorothy Parker. Reprinted by permission of The Viking Press, Inc.

[10] *Op. cit.*, pp. 22, 25.

[11] *The Church's Witness to God's Design*, Vol. II of *Man's Disorder and God's Design* ("Amsterdam Assembly Series" [New York: Harper & Row, Publishers, 1949]), p. 83. Used by permission of Student Christian Movement Press, Ltd.

of Communist ethics, a part of the Nazi ideology, and the battle cry of the most cynical forces in American politics; it has won wide acceptance among otherwise loyal and enlightened churchmen. Those in Wisconsin churches who opposed Senator Joseph McCarthy's campaign for a second term because his brutal and cynical methods seemed to defy the basic elements of Christian conviction were often told: "It is a sad mistake to oppose McCarthy. His methods may be regrettably wrong, but he is doing an essential work. Someone must oppose the Communists in public life, and if he often misstates the facts, you must remember that he fights adversaries who make lying a basic strategy. It is so important to defeat Communism that the end justifies the means." Too late these churchmen discovered that what the Senator stood for was a greater danger to American democracy than what he opposed and had an acceptance within American life—and so a capacity to divide and corrupt—which his opponents never could achieve. McCarthyism has passed off the scene, but its potential dangers still endure; for the virus which carried the disease is still harbored in this mood which accepts the cry that the end justifies the means.

A fourth mood is fear: fear of Communism, of the atom, of the darker races. More pervasive than these specific fears, and giving them their power to strike panic, is the nameless anxiety which lives in large numbers of people. Unable to say what they fear, they are tormented by a torturing, nerve-straining, strength-sapping dread of the unknown. While it is true that we are afraid because the times are dangerous, it is also true that the times are dangerous because we are afraid. As Robert Frost put it, "There is nothing I am afraid of like scared people." A frightened man is an unpredictable man. A fear-filled public has steadily whittled down the area of its civil liberties, repeatedly bartering a little more freedom for some desired security.

A final mood is worth noting: the painful sense of having

lost our identity. Arthur Miller's play, *Death of a Salesman*, owed no small part of its phenomenal public reception to the fact that most of us could see something of ourselves reflected in its winsome, tragic central figure, Willy Loman. It is significant that the final interpretation of Willy Loman's character is given, just before the final curtain, by his son Biff who says of him: "He never knew who he was." Earlier in the play, Willy Loman had said much the same thing about his own bewilderment with life: "I still feel—kind of temporary about myself." [12] This uncertainty, running like a thread through the literature of recent decades, wins its popular response because it speaks to an answering uncertainty in many readers. Unsure what life means or of their relation to a dependable Ground of Being and often verbalizing reasonably orthodox beliefs but feeling no depth of certainty about them as the working basis of daily living, their mood becomes a despairing lostness—"I still feel—kind of temporary about myself."

He who would present the Christian message with some effective meeting of minds must grasp the central issues of the day, speak with sensitive awareness of individual persons, and understand both the issues and the persons against the background of these prevailing moods.

V

The cross of Christ speaks with power to just such moods. It challenges the assumptions of "salvation by survey." Before the cross every man must see himself as personally responsible and personally addressed even as Sir John Stainer has the chorus sing at the climax of *The Crucifixion:* "Is it nothing to you, all ye that pass by?" The crucifixion is the sad record of those who shifted responsibility—from the Sanhedrin to Pilate; from Pilate to Herod; from Herod back to Pilate; from Pilate, washing his hands, to the people. Only at one point in

[12] Act 1, from *Arthur Miller's Collected Plays* (New York: The Viking Press, Inc., 1957), p. 159.

the tragic succession is there refusal to pass the responsibility further: Jesus took it upon himself. So it is not surprising that at their post-resurrection meeting when Peter turned from the forecast of his own martyrdom to ask concerning John's responsibility, " 'What about him, Lord?' Jesus replied, '. . . what does that matter to you? Follow me yourself' " (John 21:21-22 Moffatt).

The cross speaks also to the mood of the weary idealist. Judas may have been one of these—a fanatical zealot who had joined the disciple band in the hope of the Messianic revolution which would establish the long lost national independence and who made his final desperate move in the despairing hope that he might salvage something from what looked to him increasingly like a lost cause. Peter, too, exhibited brave idealism in the upper room, as he declared, "Even though they all fall away, I will not. . . . If I must die with you, I will not deny you" (Mark 14:29, 31). Yet he retreated ignominiously. The cross makes clear that we and our idealisms are not the saviors of the world; there is but one Savior. Judas of the weary idealism could not make his way back to Jesus and died by his own hand, while Peter learned in time that though ideals cannot save, those who are forgiven and renewed by the one Savior can then be used mightily for the world's salvation.

The cross speaks to those who suppose that the end justifies the means. This was the philosophy of Caiaphas: "It is expedient." "It is expedient for you," he said, "that one man should die for the people, and that the whole nation should not perish." (John 11:50.) The high end of the nation justified what might be a distasteful, even shameful plot against one man—particularly if the one man was not Caiaphas! Likewise, Pilate sought justice for the accused until the cry was raised, "If you release this man, you are not Caesar's friend" (John 19:12). At that hoarse shout, ends came in view which made Pilate feel that even the despicable means of this unjust crucifixion would be justified. Only one figure in the whole scene rejected that mood. In a straight line all the way from the wilderness temptations, where he refused to compromise with the devil's means for achieving the lofty end of the benevolent rule of kingdoms, his steadfast refusals had rejected it.

The cross speaks to our fears. For underlying them is the suspicion that life is devoid of meaning, the world is out of control, and the forces of cynical nothingness have the last word. There is only chance, as when we say, "His number was up"; or fate, as when we sing, "Whatever will be, will be"; or necessity, as in cause producing effect in an unbreakable chain about which we can do nothing. Then we come to the cross and see that, though the forces of nothingness had their way from dawn to dark of that frightful day, God was preparing another day so that in the end the world was not out of control but "God was in Christ reconciling the world to himself" (II Cor. 5:19). There was purpose in it all, and the last word lay with God whose love still sustains us and whose "perfect love casts out fear" (I John 4:18).

So the cross speaks at last to those who feel temporary about themselves. In this crucified figure of Christ—winsome, compelling, so secure in his relation to all that is finally real that even death cannot hold him—we see the indication of what our lives centrally mean. For, as Paul put it, God intended him to "be the firstborn among many brethren" (Rom. 8:29). Who am I? A sinner, guilty of exactly such sins as put him there. But the cross tells me, too, that I am a forgiven sinner whose identity is best seen in the light of a high destiny: "Beloved, we are God's children now; it does not yet appear what we shall be, but we know that when he appears we shall be like him, for we shall see him as he is" (I John 3:2).

In the last four chapters of this book we shall explore contemporary moods in further detail, seeking ways to interpret the Christian message to the persons they possess. First, however, it is important to trace some principles which guide the thinking that undergirds preaching in such a time. In this task

27

the essential first step is to discover the theological bond between authority and communication, and to this we direct our attention in the next chapter.

For Further Study

1. Subjects opened in these chapters will repay the reflection which further reading can stimulate. To each chapter a few reading suggestions are appended, the attempt being not to give an extensive bibliography but to indicate a few books particularly pertinent and helpful. To put horizons around "achieving a meeting of minds," the following are noteworthy:

Jackson, Edgar N. A Psychology for Preaching. Great Neck, New York: Channel Press, Inc., 1961.

Luccock, Halford E. Communicating the Gospel. New York: Harper and Brothers, 1954.

Pike, James A. A New Look in Preaching. New York: Charles Scribner's Sons, 1961.

Sittler, Joseph. The Ecology of Faith. Philadelphia: Muhlenberg Press, 1961.

2. One learns much about preaching by penetrating the paragraphs of published sermons to reach into the workshop minds of the preachers who produced them. Harry Emerson Fosdick is without a peer in preaching that engages the responsive activity of the hearer's (or reader's) mind. Try reading half a dozen of his sermons (the most representative collection is contained in his Riverside Sermons [New York: Harper and Brothers, 1958]; for each sermon jot down answers to these questions:

Does the introduction make me feel that the matter under consideration is important to me? If so, what specific steps or methods evoke this response?

Does this sermon give me the impression that the preacher is thinking for me, or with me? What devices achieve this effect? What questions are raised? How does he attempt to anticipate my responses?

Does the preacher seem to have achieved empathy with those to whom he speaks? Does he tell me how I should face life, or draw me into a search for ways in which we can face it victoriously? How, specifically, does he do this?

Does the sermon provide a permissive atmosphere in which those who cannot talk back are encouraged to feel back? Note particular things said, or specific methods of expression, that make this possible.

You will find such an analysis of Dr. Fosdick's skill in making the sermon a co-operative enterprise doubly illuminating if in connection with it you read his exposition of his "project method" of preaching. First published in *Harper's Magazine*, July, 1928, it was made permanently available in the autobiography, *The Living of These Days* (New York: Harper and Brothers, 1956), pp. 92-101.

3. Before outlining your next sermon, make a list of the names or initials of six to a dozen persons with whom you have had significant contact in the past week, setting opposite each a phrase or sentence notation of a need you sensed in him. Re-examine your scripture and subject asking, "What can this mean to each of these persons at the point of his need?" Jot down the answers on paper and keep them before you in your preparation. Make your developing sermon an attempt to think with these persons in "animated conversation."

2
authority and communication

In much contemporary preaching two elements which belong organically to each other have come apart. There is no dearth of preaching brilliant in its mastery of the communicative arts but without a convincing ring of authority, nor are preachers wanting who speak with material-centered impressiveness but without depth of communication to the hearer. What is commonly wanting is the capacity to bring these vital factors together. In Phillips Brooks's classic definition, "Preaching is the communication of truth by man to men . . . the bringing of truth through personality." [1] Large numbers of ministers, losing sight of the unique nature of the truth to which Brooks referred, have laid emphasis on the communicative personality with vague religiousness or generalized good will as the truth to be conveyed. Reacting against this, others have grown so authoritarian in the presentation of the specific message that, absorbed in the content to be delivered, they have lost the capacity to communicate as "man to men."

During this decade of crowded churches it has been easy for ministers to continue in blindness to the fatal lack. If the presidential address to the 1955 Assembly of the National Council of Churches was accurate, however, in drawing the picture of "humanistic nationalism" as America's predominant religious ideology, the popularity of church attendance is no certain symbol of the effectiveness of the pulpit in communicating the gospel. Referring to this popular religion as an amalgam of faith in science, common sense, the Golden Rule, sportsmanship, and individual independence, the National Council president declared that the average American's god

[1] *Lectures on Preaching* (London: H. R. Allenson, 1902), p. 5.

is no transcendent being on whom one utterly depends and to whom he gives unqualified commitment. Rather he is a convenience alternately to be used for one's own ends and blamed when affairs do not turn out to one's liking.[2]

There is evidence that the picture is not overdrawn. Crowded churches in the time of the ascendancy of such an ideology raise questions as to whether preaching has not either communicated a generalized religiousness which creates little tension with this mood or presented a more particularized and demanding message in a way that failed to establish persuasive communication.

Uneasiness grows on the minister as to whether he is fulfilling his function. Kyle Haselden suggests editorially that preachers have lost their true identity. From this "spiritual amnesia," he believes three consequences have ensued—"the ministerial Accent on Amiability," "the Resort to Sentimentality," and "the ministerial Addiction to Activity." It is a sorry picture of a pulpit in which authority and communication have lost touch with each other.

As might be expected in an age of communication, there is much skillful use of communicative devices. Often such skills have become the principal feature of the preaching. A sermon by a prominent minister on a nationwide network began with a text from Eph. 4:13—"until we all attain to . . . mature manhood, to the measure of the stature of the fulness of Christ"—and proceeded to develop a message on maturity in terms of key points gleaned from the reading of Harry Overstreet. The work was brilliantly done. The materials sparkled. The devices for fitting smoothly into the comfortable grooves of the popular mind were aptly wrought. But there was no authoritatively distinctive ring of the Christian gospel. Maturity was discussed; maturity *in Christ* was lost. Another sermon recently published began with an extended summary of Rabbi Liebman's *Peace of Mind*, for which it then claimed

[2] Eugene Carson Blake, as quoted in Martin E. Marty, *The New Shape of American Religion* (New York: Harper & Row, Publishers, 1959), p. 77.

the endorsement of Jesus by identifying it with his "Peace I leave with you" (John 14:27). Still another recent volume of pulpit material contained a sermon chapter on "Christ and Your Health" which lost any distinctive message of its own by crowding its pages with sixteen quotations from secular authors, seventeen assorted New Testament passages, illustrative material used without direct quotation from six other sources, and an appeal for support by a name-dropping device from a long list of classic writers merely mentioned in passing.

Such preaching displays admirable virtuosity in the arts of getting and holding attention and finding common ground with the interests of the listener. For all this, however, it does not finally communicate. Its message is not sufficiently distinctive to carry the authoritative note of the gospel. The contemporary preacher must project his message into the teeth of the gale of the mass media. The air is full of voices. The age of communication is also the age of sensation, each crisis made to seem more startling than the last. Strangely, it is the age of forgetfulness as well, this week's big story crowding last week's out of mind. So it becomes the age of apathy; a public acclimated to crisis and exhausted by hysteria loses sensitivity and the will to respond. For preaching in such a time, facile skills in communication are not enough. Only the distinctive voice can be heard or remembered. The preacher who speaks brightly gets passing notice and quick forgetfulness as one voice in the general din; only he whose message carries some sense of the weight of authority rooted in a vital gospel communicates meaning which endures.

The lot of the preacher who takes his stand on authoritative content in his message is no better. Centered in content, he does not reach his people with the persuasiveness of those who get *inside their minds*. His preoccupation with content, to the exclusion of concern for real personal contact, makes him an alien voice speaking from a distance. He may declare his message with the power of a coldly intellectual process which wins respect for his thought, but this cannot assure acceptance for his gospel. The pulpit has strengths and weaknesses of its own, different from those of the printed page. The argument which carries conviction in print may not persuade from the pulpit; for the sermon is an auditory experience which must be grasped by the mind at the moment of hearing or not at all. The listener to a sermon cannot go his own pace, as does the reader of a book, but must travel at the preacher's pace or be lost. No matter how authoritative the intellectual process, if the communicative aids are inadequate the case is lost.

Much has been gained by the current emphasis on proclamation. It has reminded those who preach that they are not purveyors of good advice, nor reviewers of popular books, nor pleaders for generalized and often sentimental good will. They are not exhorters lashing men with imperatives; nor are they "poets of the mighty dream" dealing in the conditional if-world of the subjunctive. Their native mood is the indicative. They announce. They state. We have gained much by a re-emphasis of the proclamation of the mighty acts of God in Christ.

The recovery of this note, however, is not without danger. To many minds proclamation is easily identified with mere statement which men may take or leave, the outcome being no concern of the preacher's. This danger is inherent in the kind of forceful statement which Roy Pearson lays down as the baseline for his consideration of the purpose of preaching. Proclamation, he emphasizes, is so singly the goal of preaching that "it is unconcerned about any results" beyond getting its objective word heard and understood. So seen, he declares, the sermon ceases to be a means and becomes an end. One can no more ask why there is a sermon than why there is God.[3]

It should be said that Dr. Pearson has the balanced judgment to acknowledge later in the same book that the preacher has some other responsibilities, and that if preaching changes

[3] *The Ministry of Preaching* (New York: Harper & Row, Publishers, 1959), p. 15 f.

nothing, the preaching should be changed. For the less balanced or mature, however, a preoccupation with proclamation is a secure haven from the agonizing responsibility to get the message planted deep in the motivating centers of men's lives —a responsibility calling for craftsmanship in communication won only at painful cost.

Communicative skills are not optional electives for the preacher who would have his message carry authority. Content-centered preaching becomes authoritarian rather than authoritative; and for men of this age the authoritarian seldom commands final allegiance. This generation has seen too many once-final judgments set aside. Reviewing one of the shocks in his own intellectual history, Alfred North Whitehead serves as spokesman of the mood with which the minister must conduct his dialogue. The Newtonian physics, Whitehead recalls, once taught as whole truth, still possesses a working usefulness but is no longer true in the way his earlier teachers represented it.[4]

To an age thus disillusioned about what had seemed compelling authority, authoritarian proclamation means little. So long as the preacher's voice comes with coercive insistence from without, it wins little real response. Only as the preacher sufficiently understands the conditions of communication necessary to win the identifying response of the listener can he be deeply persuasive. Empathy, a familiar concept in counseling, is too much neglected in preaching.

A sermon based on the capacity of the preacher to feel his way inside the hearer may lift men to insights, convictions, and new patterns of behavior to which no authoritarian word spoken from a lofty height could have driven them. The listener to such preaching is gripped by a message which comes with the compelling force of his own awakened insight. He has the impression not so much of being told by a voice from

[4] Lucien Price (ed.), *The Dialogues of Alfred North Whitehead* (Boston: Little, Brown & Co., 1954), p. 238.

without, as of responding to something newly formed within.[5] Such preaching achieves real authority by relinquishing any authoritarian claim.

Here then is the paradox of preaching: centering on communication to the neglect of authority, it fails to communicate; majoring in authority at the cost of careful communication, it ceases to be authoritative.

II

In the face of his peculiar temptations, let the facile practitioner of the communicative arts find the authority which inheres in his calling to preach. For the sermon is not so much something said as something done. It is a man's act; but, if it be real preaching, it is more especially God's act. Early in the present century P. T. Forsyth reminded preachers that Protestant worship must remain at a disadvantage by comparison with the Roman mass as long as men came from mass with a sense of something done in the spirit-world, and from a Protestant service impressed only with something said to the present world.[6] Preaching which allows bright rhetorical devices to take the place of a forthright message confesses, by its self-consciously nervous appeal for approval, that it has already met this defeat.

Any adequate theology of preaching builds on the conviction that God not only commissions and sends preachers; he is himself present in true preaching. Whatever the date or origin of the supplied ending of The Gospel According to Mark, the faith of the church speaks through its declaration: "And they went forth and preached everywhere, while the Lord worked with them and confirmed the message by the signs that attended it" (Mark 16:20). This was but the confirmation of the promise given with the church's commission: "Go therefore and make disciples of all nations . . . and lo,

[5] Cf. May, op. cit., p. 124.
[6] Positive Preaching and the Modern Mind (Cincinnati: Jennings and Graham, 1907), p. 81.

I am with you always, to the close of the age" (Matt. 28:19a, 20b). It is the faith authorized by the Christ of the Fourth Gospel, who declared that the Counselor, the Spirit of Truth, "will take what is mine and declare it to you" (John 16:14). The faith of the church held that Pentecost was not a victory of Peter's eloquent words which God incidentally approved, but God's act through the Holy Spirit using Peter's words as an instrument.

This faith endures in the church. A contemporary master preacher and evangelist, D. T. Niles, confesses that though he has labored to speak God's word as it has come to him, the listener can hear God's word not because the preacher has spoken it but only because God has spoken it. We cannot say God's word, Dr. Niles reminds us. Only God can do that. But amazingly God sometimes makes our words the medium through which his word becomes active in another's heart.[7] Not what we say, but what God does, is finally important.

W. B. J. Martin declares that a typical sermon of today is a closely linked argument when it ought to be a vivid firsthand experience.[8] In the light of a New Testament theology of preaching his distinction is not between two kinds of sermon but between a sermon and a religious speech. In preaching something *happens*: God encounters men. John Knox underscores this point as he asserts that when preaching fails it is not for lack of learning or of any other human quality we like to attribute to it. The fatal lack is that there is no channeling of God's power to the hearers. There is expression of a man's thought of whatever quality. But God's present act is missing. Words are spoken, but no event occurs. The mighty act of God in Christ is not present.[9]

To say that preaching is not argument but event is to say

---

[7] *Preaching the Gospel of the Resurrection* (Philadelphia: The Westminster Press, 1954), p. 22 f.

[8] Quoted in Donald Macleod, *Word and Sacrament* (Englewood Cliffs, N. J.: Prentice-Hall, Inc., 1960), p. 12.

[9] *The Integrity of Preaching* (Nashville: Abingdon Press, 1957), p. 93 f.

that through it the supreme event finds continuance as the cross extends its reach in time. What happened on Calvary was unique and unrepeatable. Paul declares that the death Christ "died he died to sin, once for all" (Rom. 6:10), and the Epistle to the Hebrews underscores that "Christ, having been offered once to bear the sins of many, will appear a second time, not to deal with sin but to save those who are eagerly waiting for him" (9:28). Yet the sacrifice once offered reaches into our lives through preaching. Any minister who has long preached can recall times when someone has said, "What great, good news that is! I never realized it before." Yet the surprising news was just the old story of God's love and forgiveness made vivid on the cross. Heard innumerable times before, it had found its mark on this particular day not because of greater eloquence or a more persuasive argument, but by reason of a new readiness which the event finally touched. The important thing was not that something had been said, but that a person who had previously heard the words now was touched by the act. A divine encounter had taken place.

Nothing will save real preaching for the man who has lost its distinctive thrust through preoccupation with communicative techniques short of the realization that he participates in this divine event.

If the communication-minded preacher can be rescued only by discovering this theological dimension of preaching as event, his brother minister who loses persuasive contact with people by a too exclusive attention to content likewise stands in need of a theological salvation, a serious facing of the nature of revelation.

The preacher must take seriously the growing theological consensus that what is revealed is not propositions about God, but God himself. As there may be wave phenomena but no sound unless there is an ear to hear and no teaching unless there is learning, there cannot be revelation unless there is appropriation. Let the preacher ask in deep seriousness, What

does this mean to the act of preaching? If preaching participates in God's work of revelation, so understood, is it enough
that weighty things be said unless the saying so fits the necessities of mind and emotion that the way is open for appropriation and response?

Revelation as "inner history," in the sense in which
H. Richard Niebuhr speaks of it, has profound implications
for preaching. It is not *history* which conveys revelation, but
history appropriated as "my history." So appropriated, history
served as the medium of the New Testament revelation. The
writers returned in memory to the crucial events through
which, confronted by another on whom they deeply depended,
they came to a new kind of awareness of themselves. Reliving
the memory of a past which continued in them, they came to
a new life.[10] "Our fathers," "our Lord," "our God"—through
these significant identifications the church learned to see itself
and its faith. Thus the Deuteronomic writer identified himself
with the men of the Exodus to declare: "Not with our fathers
did the Lord make this covenant, but with us, who are all of
us here alive this day" (Deut. 5:3). Thus the devout Jew
celebrating the Passover in any age is commanded in Exodus:
"And you shall tell your son on that day, 'It is because of what
the Lord did for me when I came out of Egypt'" (Exod. 13:
8). It is this intense appropriation of the biblical events as
our history which enables them to serve as revelation. When
this happens they hold the key to life. In Niebuhr's telling
figure, revelation is like a luminous sentence in a difficult book
from which we read the otherwise elusive meaning of the
pages that went before and come after.

It is at the point where recorded history becomes any
man's inner history that the preacher is involved. Mere statement of the events is not sufficient to open the way to this
personal identification for the man whose mind is nurtured in
another culture and an alien way of looking at life. Finely

[10] *The Meaning of Revelation* (New York: The Macmillan Company,
1941), p. 72.

38

wrought theological reasoning may fall far short of the mark. Doctrinal statement, however correct and helpful to those who view the matter from inside the community of faith, may remain incomprehensible or unacceptable to the man who most needs faith's illumination. Here the literary critic may help us. At one point in his essay on "The Paradox of Religious Poetry," Charles I. Glicksberg writes that dogma as such has no place in real poetry. Only as doctrine is transformed into vision can it serve the purposes of art. The symbols employed by the authentic Christian poet penetrate beneath formulated doctrine to the experience on which it rests. Unless the poet recaptures an original vision of this intense experience he becomes an echo of a "lapsed tradition." [11]

But this need to communicate some firsthand vision, some fresh and sharply concrete apprehension of the event, is the preacher's necessity as well as the poet's. And the preacher is under a further mandate to communicate a vitally relived event not in mere finely wrought and subtle language which can be re-examined at leisure by those disposed to search its depths for meaning, but in a spoken word which grips and wins in the swift moment in which the running sound falls on the ear. He must communicate not in words only, but by the total effect of his meeting as a man with other men. Content however vital, ideas however vigorous, are not enough. Unless the preacher has been at pains to see a kindling vision with his inner eye and to body it forth in kindling form, his message does not win its way for it does not capture that place within the hearer's mind which makes it for him "internal history." What was revelation to the preacher fails to become revelation to the hearer, not for want of content but for want of concerned communication.

The second- or third-rate poet, Glicksberg observes, may weave his variations on the dogmas as tradition has delivered them, but the major poet must return to a fresh appropriation

<hr />

[11] *Literature and Religion; A Study in Conflict* (Dallas: Southern Methodist University Press, 1960), p. 83.

of the experience from which the dogma sprang. Is it too much to suggest that this may also be a mark of the difference between first-rate and second- or third-rate preaching? The failure is not in the want of brilliant thought but in the lack of return to the firsthand vision which provides a luminous capacity to help others see and receive as their own what is being talked about.

It is at this point that one fears the current stress on proclamation, which too easily becomes identified in the minds of many preachers with mere announcement. As New Testament *kerygma* is transposed into *didache*, as prophecy continues to hold its place beside these two as a recognized form of address within the church, and as Paul's public discourses on a long series of occasions recorded in Acts take on a distinctly polemic quality, the common denominator is not so much proclamation as it is address offered as a medium of encounter with God in Christ. It is impassioned and purposeful address. If Paul's epistles are any indication of the quality of his preaching, it was not nearly as devoid of eloquence as a too literal acceptance of his disclaimer in I Cor. 2 might imply. It is full of imaginative use of the Old Testament scriptures. It rings the changes on ingenious figures of speech. On occasion it builds its own apologetic structures. For all its vigorous thought it is no flatland of intellect devoid of emotion. It shouts its joy. It all but sobs its heartbreak. It bursts forth into violent denunciation. It speaks the deep tones of love. It entreats: "So we are ambassadors for Christ, God making his appeal through us. We beseech you on behalf of Christ, be reconciled to God." (II Cor. 5:20.) Proclamation there is, to be sure, but never detached or impersonal. Surely this body of letters, though not reports of the apostle's sermons, must be of one piece with the preaching of the man who most set the pattern of the church's mind and heart; and far more than objective proclamation, it is ardent invitation to encounter.

III

We have been saying that without a grasp of the distinctive and authoritative event at the heart of preaching the most artful speech may fail to communicate the gospel; and that apart from careful fulfillment of the person-centered conditions of communicative speech, authoritative statement of undeniably valid content may not awaken the shock of recognition and the surrendered response which give it real authority. There is one further step to take—the recognition that authority and communication meet in what has been well called a "double analysis" of the scriptural text. Valid preaching, as Professor John Knox points out, is not a circle drawn around a single center, either in exegesis of a biblical text or in address to contemporary need. It is rather an ellipse drawn around two foci: one in the text, the other in a current human situation.

All we have been saying implies what needs no reinforcement at this late date, that the Bible is the one indispensable source and center of preaching. This generally means that preaching is done more truly and with greater power when it takes its stance squarely within the text of a single Bible passage than when it seeks to range over the Scriptures to develop a topic. If biblical truth is not generalized essence but luminous event, this serious grappling with the text brings the preacher nearer to the real Bible message. If the preacher knows his Bible well enough to read the text in the light of its widest context, this confinement within a passage need not bias his interpretation. If he is a pastor-preacher speaking weekly to the same congregation, he can let the Word speak through this text today, assured that there will be other Sundays for other aspects of the truth. If he has, or can develop, any sense of drama he must know that the real power lies in draining the possibilities of dramatic unity in one scene, not in a hasty survey of many.

Both authority and communication begin with real *listening* to the text. Frederick W. Robertson had the secret:

Receive—imbibe—and then your mind will create. Poets are creators because they are recipients. They open their hearts to Nature instead of going to her with views of her already made and second hand; so with Scripture—patient, quiet, long, reverent listening to it; then suggestiveness. In other words, make the Word a daily meditation and the interpretation will come.[12]

The meditation comes to the text in two ways. One is the careful critical-exegetical study of the passage itself and in its context. All that the preacher can master of technical preparation for this study must be brought into play. The methods are too well known to need consideration here, but nothing else the preacher can do at other points in his preparation can make up for failure to do this work. When it is done, however, he has taken only the first step.

He must then go on to observe closely where the truth this message enbodies meets the life of his own time and people. He must be a student of his time through its literature, its thought and science, its public affairs, and most of all through his own people. As we have seen, it is a valuable exercise for the minister to list weekly on paper no less than a dozen of the people with whom he has had pastoral dealings within the past seven days, together with an articulate line which recalls to him the particular need he sensed in each of them. Let him take time to look at the text through the eyes of each of these as best his sensitive heart and trained imagination will permit. Let him look at each of them from within the text. When he has done this, he may be in a position to help them make the personal appropriation through which this scripture will become revelation for them.

For illustration of this double analysis it may be helpful to look all too briefly at Gen. 3:8-19, which the preacher might approach through the dramatic text, "But the Lord God called to the man, and said to him, 'Where are you?' And he said, 'I heard the sound of thee in the garden, and I was afraid, be-

---

[12] Quoted in Macleod, op. cit., p. 32.

cause I was naked; and I hid myself' " (3:9-10). Our own aloneness and the despair many of us feel of making ourselves understood speaks through this passage. Our human relationships keep breaking down at cost of loneliness, failure, and the colossal threats that loom on the world's horizon. Is there any hope that we can deal with them?

Hendrik Kraemer has suggested that this chapter offers the answer. Broken is the fundamental relationship to God on which all other relationships depend. Having first violated his relation to God, the man in flight from God finds disruption on every hand. First there is self-justification by accusing God —"The woman whom *thou* gavest to be with me, she gave me fruit of the tree, and I ate" (italics mine, Gen. 3:12). The deepest human relation, that between husband and wife, is disrupted. Work, intended to be a blessing, is vitiated as the soil itself comes under a curse. The relation of brothers is violated as Cain murders Abel. Even the basic bond of language is broken. Words, meant to convey meaning, are twisted to distort it as Cain replies to God's question about Abel: "I know not where he is. Am I my brother's keeper?" [13]

So much for the direct look at the text. For want of a parish in which to see the personal needs and denials which speak to the text and to which it speaks, let us look at the well-drawn characters in Keith Wheeler's *Peaceable Lane*.[14] Central to the action is Matt Jones, an ordinary man who has taken good will for granted without dedication to any specific causes. Matt's quiet suburban street, Peaceable Lane, has its share of petty people with the usual reservations about each other; but for the most part they live in neighborly tolerance touched with some good will—except for Bronson, who for years has kept up a constant mutual grudge with the neighborhood in general.

The sudden, devastating crisis descends on the lane in

[13] Hendrik Kraemer, *The Communication of the Christian Faith* (Philadelphia: The Westminster Press, 1956), p. 18 f.
[14] (New York: Simon and Schuster, Inc., 1960), p. 137.

the form of hysteria born of the news that Bronson is selling his place to a Negro. None of the neighbors has seen the buyer; no one knows his name. It is enough that he is a Negro. In a hasty neighborhood meeting they decide to pool their funds though none of them can afford it, and buy the place at a premium to keep the intruder out. Dr. Abram, a refugee from Vienna, casts his vote with reluctance because it is a violation of his Jewish principles, but with decisiveness because as a Jew he has suffered in Vienna and he has not the courage to face great risk again. Estelle Outerbridge makes a plea against this violation of human right in the name of her Christian faith, but is overruled by her husband. Zack Gold reflects the struggle between his fear and his tortured conscience, forced to "make a choice of what to betray." Yet he joins the conspiracy.

After days of intrigue and violence the deal is consummated and the neighborhood syndicate buys Bronson's house and sees him move away. They have faced a common fear, plotted together, taken risks together, won a victory together —yet it has not brought them together. On the contrary, all keep more to themselves; rumors and mutual suspicions multiply among them.

Is there a symbol of their basic alienation in the never-used fireplace they found in Bronson's home as they went in to inspect what they had bought? The house showed mute signs of the life of the family—all of it, that is, except the fireplace. It, obviously, had never held a fire. There was pathos in its bricks, as white as when the mason laid them. Matt reflected on every man's almost instinctive urge to light a fire in his place and so make it his own. In eight years, Matt thought, Bronson had not thus taken possession of this house. This had been his residence but never a place in which he was really settled.

Alienation from one another; from an unknown stranger; from their avowed faiths; and, if this symbol is taken seriously, from the Ground of Being had disrupted their Eden. Was not the last named disruption of longest standing and the primal disorder?

Then Matt discovers that the Negro buyer they have excluded is Lamar Winter, with whom he has long been closely associated in his work and whom—within the structured world of business—he considers his friend. The remainder of the novel unfolds the story of the risks Matt takes to make the house available to Winter and to attempt to make a place for him and his family in the life of the neighborhood, as well as of the community's bitter conspiracy of persecution. In the end it is Lamar Winter himself who saves the neighborhood from worse danger and dies in the act of doing so.

Perhaps that hint of a savior figure—a modern spurned and persecuted victim whose vicarious death brings the neighborhood back together—is the pointer to what the Genesis story needs for its completion. For there men lost their relationship to each other and to the world itself when they broke their relationship with God; and God could not speak his final saving word until he spoke it from the Cross.

So the possibilities of the preaching message begin to emerge. The analysis of the text alone does not supply it. The analysis of contemporary life, in the parish or in the novel, does not provide it. But when the two analyses speak to each other, a theme and a message begin to come in view. Authority and communication stand in mutual support. This process of double analysis will meet us again and again as we search for the path to the controlling centers of the contemporary mind. We must now inquire more carefully what we mean when we speak of preaching as encounter.

For Further Study

1. A number of recent books have probed the theological bond between authority and communication. None has displaced Forsyth's *Positive Preaching and the Modern Mind* (cf. footnote 1 above), a work which towers with more heroic stature as the years go on. Among newer publications, the following will provoke creative reflection from varied viewpoints:

Kraemer, Hendrik. *The Communication of the Christian Faith.* Philadelphia: The Westminster Press, 1956.

Macleod, Donald. *Word and Sacrament.* Englewood Cliffs, N. J.: Prentice Hall, Inc., 1960.

Smith, Charles W. F. *Biblical Authority for Modern Preaching.* Philadelphia: The Westminster Press, 1960.

Ritschl, Dietrich. *A Theology of Proclamation.* Richmond: John Knox Press, 1960.

2. In Chapter Six of his *Prophetic Preaching* (Nashville: Abingdon Press, 1958) Otto Baab suggested some approaches, resembling what we have called double analysis, to contemporary problems in conjunction with Old Testament passages. In your notebook begin your own double analysis of these passages.

(a) Study the passage in its biblical context to see what light is thrown on the situation to which it was addressed.

(b) Go to your commentaries for help in the exegesis of the passage itself.

(c) Note how Professor Baab approached the passage in the light of the confluence of a problem of our time with the need to which the passage was first addressed.

(d) Write out your current week's list of individuals in whom you sense personal needs, and what—in the light of the foregoing steps—the passage can say personally to each of them.

(e) You will now have before you a mass of material better for your situation than any book of preaching helps could supply; study this material with care and from it begin to articulate a sermon idea and work out an outline..

3. From your devotional reading of the Bible enter in your notebook passages in which you see possibilities of double analysis emerging. Apply to them such study as is suggested in the foregoing paragraph. Such a notebook will be a rich resource for future preaching.

3
dynamic encounter

When we characterize preaching as essentially a summons to encounter with God, it is important that we say, with such precision as we can, what we mean. Encounter is more than meeting. Dictionary definitions point to "a meeting in conflict" or "an unexpected meeting." Biblical references to proclamation indicate that these elements of conflict or surprise were present when the prophets and apostles preached.

In his pioneer work on *The Apostolic Preaching*,[1] Charles H. Dodd traced out the *kerygma* as a message with typical and somewhat uniform content. His focus on the Greek noun meaning proclamation pointed a direction which other scholars have followed in quest of the preached word that underlies the New Testament. Recent studies have turned attention to the parallel Greek verb *kerussein*, and its use in both the New Testament and the Septuagint. This redirection of attention to the verb commonly translated "to herald," "to proclaim," "to preach," brings the purpose of preaching as dynamic encounter more fully into view.

In typical Old Testament usage this verb appears in the account of the presentation of Joseph to the people as prime minister: "and they cried before him, 'Bow the knee'" (Gen. 41:43). No mere announcement of the new leader's arrival; this cry of the herald summoned the people to give him their allegiance. Having read the events of his time as signs of the approaching day of the Lord, Joel uses the verb *kerussein* in his appeal, "call a solemn assembly" (Joel 1:14). There is impassioned urgency in his call to encounter with God whose

---

[1] New York: Harper & Row, Publishers, 1936.

day of judgment is at hand. Urgency, indeed, is the note characteristic of the uses of *kerussein* by the prophets, whether they are dealing with a national emergency or heralding the messianic ministry.[2]

With an urgent summons to encounter—"Repent, for the kingdom of heaven is at hand" (Matt. 3:2)—John the Baptist began the preaching of the New Testament period. As Jesus used *kerussein*, it involved a call to decision.[3] He commissioned the disciples to announce the new age: "Preach as you go, saying, 'The kingdom of heaven is at hand' " (Matt. 10:7). The purpose of the proclamation as summons to encounter is clearly stated: "He who receives you receives me, and he who receives me receives him who sent me" (Matt. 10:40).

A vital reemphasis upon the essential nature of preaching as bringing men face to face with God's Word through the proclamation of the biblical message runs through the thinking of the years since World War I. Karl Barth has spoken of God's revelation as reaching men in three forms: the proclaimed Word, the written Word, and the revealed Word.[4] This relationship of preaching to its roots in the Bible appropriated as revelation is lost only at peril of emptying the message of its validity. It is imperative, however, that the preacher keep clearly before him not only the biblical *content* of the message but the *objective* of the proclamation, as does Donald Miller when he writes: "To preach is to bear witness to the unique action of God in Jesus Christ as it is set forth in the record of that action—the Bible—*so that the judgment and redemption enacted in those historic deeds become current realities to the soul.*"[5] In this definition, the biblical source and the outcome in the facing of God's acts as "current

---

[2] Robert H. Mounce, *The Essential Nature of New Testament Preaching* (Grand Rapids: Wm. B. Eerdmans Publishing Co., 1960), p. 18.

[3] *Ibid.*, p. 37.

[4] *Church Dogmatics* (New York: Charles Scribner's Sons, 1936), Vol. I, Part I, pp. 98-140.

[5] *The Way to Biblical Preaching* (Nashville: Abingdon Press, 1957), p. 24. Italics mine.

realities to the soul" are the two poles between which the dynamics of the encounter flow. If either pole were removed, true preaching would cease. We are brought thus to our working definition: *Preaching is a divine-human act in which men in their lostness are summoned to a saving encounter with God's Word through the spoken words of a convinced witness.*

The biblical message is not for the most part a confirmation of our opinions and purposes, as Isaiah saw:

> For my thoughts are not your thoughts,
>   neither are your ways my ways, says the Lord.
> —Isa. 55:8

Christian faith rises out of this tension and lives under its stress so that Paul could say with dramatic intensity, "The world has been crucified to me, and I to the world" (Gal. 6:14). To preach the gospel is to speak into this tension, even to heighten it. For when its news reaches a man—the preacher no less than those in the pews—it so addresses him as to awaken what Paul Tillich has called "infinite concern." When we are concerned about something, Tillich points out, "we are involved in it, . . . a part of ourselves is in it, . . . we participate with our hearts." Indeed we participate anxiously.[6] Unless something has happened in this dimension of ultimate concern, it may be doubted whether men have really heard the gospel.

To meet with God in Christ is to be confronted by deep and costly challenge; in aspects of our own existence, in awareness of human need, in issues with the world around us, to be involved with anxious concern. To the degree that we have died to the world, we live with Christ. We are born into new life by the dynamics of this costly encounter.

II

Halford E. Luccock once pictured a Sunday morning churchgoer as hearing the lesson from the Sermon on the

---

[6] *The New Being* (New York: Charles Scribner's Sons, 1955), p. 153.

Mount while a considerable part of his mind remained busy with the report of the Stock Market. The clash between the contrasted trains of thought is startling.

> Blessed are the poor in spirit for theirs is the kingdom of— American Can gone up to 57. . . . Blessed are the meek—that must mean the Amalgamated are really buying into it. . . . Blessed are those that mourn—two hundred shares at ninety-seven will come to. . . . Take no thought for the morrow—I'll have to cover that drop in Consolidated Electric to-morrow or get caught short. . . . But seek ye first the kingdom of heaven.[7]

In the presence of such a colloquy, Luccock remarked, it becomes apparent that Jesus stated our own unresolved problem: "No one can serve two masters" (Matt. 6:24).

Yet two potential masters call. Christ stands over against the life of our time. H. Richard Niebuhr has observed that men of our time are offended by the very elements in the gospel which offended those of earlier centuries. Similar arguments have been directed against the faith by "ancient spiritualists and modern materialists." Religious Romans bringing charges of atheism, or more recent atheists rejecting faith in God, nationalists on the one hand and humanists on the other —from their diverse perspectives the opponents join in a common attack.[8]

Ancient Romans objected to the new faith because, as Gibbon said, Christians were "animated by a contempt for present existence and by confidence in immortality." This is still an offense to men absorbed in the preoccupations of this world, who reject the idea of immortality and hold in contempt a faith which they fear will divert attention from what they regard to be of primary importance. Christianity, they aver, calls men to rely on the grace of God rather than on human achievement; and, convinced that our own achieve-

[7] *Jesus and the American Mind* (New York: The Abingdon Press, 1930), p. 128.

[8] *Christ and Culture* (New York: Harper & Row, Publishers, 1951), p. 5.

ment is all we can depend on, they hold such faith to be a dangerous illusion. Christ and his church, they charge, intolerantly demand exclusive belief in him; this is shocking to an age which holds that what a man believes matters little, so long as he believes intensely in something. Sharing the eclecticism of the Hollywood star who declared, "I believe in everything a little bit," this popular tolerance justifies the attempt to build life on a harmonization of opposites—pleasure without principle, wealth without work, love without loyalty, democracy without dignity. They pronounce the Christian doctrine of forgiveness false on the grounds that to forgive is to short-circuit justice and relieve men of responsibility for their deeds.

In all this it is plain that Christ's encounter with the world is one of such mutual challenge that if preaching is to fulfill its function, the preacher must have a secure stance in his understanding of the relationship between the two poles of the dynamic situation in which he participates. Niebuhr studied five forms of this relation which we shall recount briefly, though not quite in the order in which he enumerates them and without attempting to summarize his exposition.

The first of these finds "Christ against culture." For our generation the antipathy grows obvious as the attack is pressed simultaneously from several directions. Communism opposes him with its denial of God, its centering of concern in the production and distribution of material goods, its substitution of the messiahship of the masses, and its foreshortening of hope to salvation in the utopia of a classless society brought about by the dialectic of history. Western materialism denies him less obviously but with effects often more deadly because less apparent. Scientism presumes to replace him with salvation through human engineering which promises to deliver not only the means but the goals of the good life by the application of scientific method. Rival world religions, awakened to new missionary activity, bid for the loyalties of men; and

Islam now outpaces Christianity in its spread across Africa.[9] The seemingly irreconcilable conflict led such men as Tolstoi to reject the present world in a valiant attempt to give exclusive loyalty to Christ.

For most men this solution in terms of mutually exclusive alternatives will seem neither possible nor wise. Even Tolstoi could not make it complete, and his personal renunciation served only to transfer to his wife the burden of managing their estates. For the preacher, culture is the medium of interpretation. Language, history, literature, the fine arts—all manifestations of culture—provide the channels of communication. From a biblical viewpoint culture is no stranger to God's will. Having been placed in a world of God's making and of which the Creator said that it was very good (Gen. 1:31), man was commanded to "fill the earth and subdue it" (Gen. 1:28). Man was invited by his Creator to name all the creatures (Gen. 2:19), which in biblical idiom is a way of saying that God intended man to understand their meaning and nature. By definition culture is this understanding of and dominion over the created world coming to its fullest and most refined expression. In the biblical conception of the Fall, the blight of man's sin rests upon nature itself (Gen. 3:17-18); but the repudiation of nature and consequently of culture is not absolute. Jesus mingling with tax collectors and sinners, participating in the affairs of the synagogue, commending the insight of a centurion, making immortal parables from the daily affairs of common people, commending "the sons of this world" as "wiser in their own generation than the sons of light" (Luke 16:8), and accused —by contrast with the asceticism of John—as a "glutton and a drunkard" (Matt. 11:19), was undeniably a participant in culture. This full participation was part of God's strategy in assuming full humanity for our redemption: "the Word became flesh and dwelt among us" (John 1:14). For the sake of

⁹ Alan Walker, A New Mind for a New Age (Nashville: Abingdon Press, 1959), p. 137 f.

the gospel the greatest of the apostles, who could quote the Scriptures to the Jews, quote the philosophers and poets to the Greeks, use the law courts to reach the Romans, support himself in his mission through the tentmaker's trade, and give practical nautical counsel to a ship's captain, employed this divine strategy of penetrating culture. As he himself said of his work, "I have become all things to all men, that I might by all means save some. I do it all for the sake of the gospel, that I may share its blessings" (I Cor. 9:22-23). Opposition between Christ and culture there surely is, but it is scarcely of a nature so absolute as to justify the characterization of the total relationship as "Christ against culture."

Perhaps "Christ above culture" may describe a tenable relation which takes the varied strands of life in the world in any age and weaves them into such a synthesis as made the work of Thomas Aquinas a notable landmark. This possibility is suggested by the elements of good which Luccock notes in the strands of our heritage included in his whimsical construction of a scene at the opening of the will to which the twentieth century is heir. The Puritan is first to speak:

"I leave a sense of God; of responsibility to God; a tradition of duty and the high seriousness of life. I leave an inheritance of devotion to the human rights of the individual and their expression in democracy. To you also I leave, with all the conflict involved, an exaltation of material success; a sanctification of profit; a strong momentum to the acquisitive instinct which sadly belies my affirmation that the chief end of man is to 'glorify God and to enjoy him forever.' "

The Pioneer hands on his legacy: "I bequeath a wilderness subdued and conquered for civilization; a new proving ground for a new order of life. I leave you stalwart elements of social strength and a happy valiancy, a tempered fortitude and hopefulness. To you also I leave an aggressive and undisciplined individualism; a preoccupation with material things, a religion of 'getting on.' With the ironical result that, having made civilization out of the wilderness, you may now struggle with forces which threaten to make a wilderness out of civilization."

The Machine speaks: "I give you a magical fairyland of mechanical progress, but a fairyland peopled with ogres and demons. I leave you a new freedom from drudgery and a new slavery of spirit; I leave you large comforts and moral mediocrity. I leave you external riches and internal penury, giant powers and pigmy purposes. And may God have mercy on your soul!" [10]

Such a picture suggests that there is little hope of bringing the elements of the present world into a synthesis under the banner of Christ. Included with the blessings of this heritage are contradictions that give point to the question, How can you synthesize Yes and No? [11]

A third alternative might be that of "Christ and culture in paradox," which posits two centers of authority, each sovereign in its own sphere and permanently dividing control of man's allegiance. Symbolic of this paradox is the juxtaposition of the national flag and the Christian flag in many American churches, with a tendency to bring them nearer and nearer to the altar as if to suggest a twofold reality central to, if not the object of, worship. The popular urgency to place the national flag in the place of preferred honor even in the house of God—and in cases of conflict between the claims of Christ and those of the nation either to give preference to the national cause or to achieve the same result by a refusal to recognize that a conflict exists—reveals the implicit tendency of this Christ and culture paradox.

The Lutheran expression of this relation in the doctrine of the two orders lies back of the epic struggle of Martin Niemöller. This heroic Berlin pastor resisted Hitler with mighty courage when it became apparent that the dictator was infringing the specific domain reserved to the sovereignty of

[10] Op. cit., p. 94.
[11] The question paraphrases a remark made in another context in Arthur T. Hadley, *The Nation's Safety and Arms Control* (New York: The Viking Press, Inc., 1961), p. xi.

the church. The tragic fact is inescapable, however, that by that time the Nazi tyranny was too deeply entrenched to be shaken by such resistance. In the early phases of the rise of the dark forces, when determined opposition might have halted their advance, Niemöller's voice was not raised because Hitler represented a power sovereign in its own field. Thus the solution of permanent paradox proves to be open to serious question in a world where demonic forces within culture itself frequently break forth.

The relation may be "Christ the transformer of culture." The need for transformation is evidenced by violence so widespread that it seems almost a cultic center of our life. The fatal drift became apparent with the change of American attitudes during World War II when the nation, which had officially protested the saturation bombing of cities during the period of its own neutrality, descended later to the obliteration bombing in Europe, the incendiary bombing of Tokyo, and the first use of the atomic bomb in wiping out the civilian centers of Hiroshima and Nagasaki. "Avoidable, unnecessary suffering," declares Alan Walker, "has become a feature of world society." [12]

The process by which emotions are further brutalized and sensitivity is dulled is seen at work in television programs offered for juvenile audiences. A week's survey of children's programs in the Chicago area monitored 134 shows which portrayed 295 crimes of violence: 93 murders, 78 shootings, 9 kidnappings, 9 robberies, 44 gun fights, 2 knifings, 33 sluggings, 2 whiplashings, 2 poisonings, and 2 bombings. What this emotional fare may be costing the children who comprise the audience is indicated by an American Medical Association report that "crime programs made 76 per cent of a group of test children more nervous and increased their fears fivefold." [13] Even worse in the long run, a diet of such "entertain-

---

[12] *Op. cit.*, p. 106.
[13] Cf. Malcolm Boyd, *Crisis in Communication* (Garden City: Doubleday & Company, Inc., 1957), p. 30 f.

ment" presumably contributes to a further dulling of the sense of shock at human suffering and a lowering of the valuation of human life. And while some objective studies cast doubt on the power of television to *produce* attitudes corresponding to those implemented on the screen, there can be little question that such a procession of stimuli *reinforces* tendencies already at work in the viewer.[14]

A society which not only tolerates widespread violence but celebrates it as a main ingredient of its leisure-time amusement shows symptoms of a sickness so deep and pervasive as to stand in need of transformation. It is cause for encouragement that a world conscience concerning the value of a human individual came to expression in the United Nations enactment, without a single dissenting vote, of the Universal Declaration of Human Rights. That the rights enunciated are disregarded in many nations should be no ground for cynical despair. For it is also true that the Bill of Rights and the post–Civil War amendments to the Constitution of the United States, though they have had a much longer period in which to establish their authority, are still too widely violated; yet they articulate the nation's conscience and provide a basis in law for the protection of civil liberties. Prior to the enactment of the Universal Declaration of Human Rights there had been no single expression of the conscience of mankind to which all nations joined in paying even lip service. Upon this declaration a further structure of world law can be erected.

Yet it is clear that even a structure such as this is powerless to transform the world if the will to observe its mandate is lacking. The sickness of the time requires healing at centers deeper than declarations and legal conventions can touch. It is the Christian conviction that Christ alone can confront culture with a power that provides this transformation. To discharge his task of releasing the dynamics inherent in the encounter, the Christian interpreter needs constantly to sharp-

---

[14] Joseph T. Klapper, *The Effects of Mass Communication* (Glencoe, Illinois: Free Press of Glencoe, Inc., 1960), p. 8.

en his awareness of the world to which the message is directed and to find his way to a firm faith-stance among the complex relationships between Christ and the culture of his own period.

III

One relation is so crucial in its challenge as to require special consideration. Described by Niebuhr as "the Christ of culture," it can be symbolized by the portrayal of our Lord in Bruce Barton's book, *The Man Nobody Knows*.[15] Barton pictured Jesus as an aggressively active, constantly busy leader versed in the art of public relations and vigorous in its practice. His manipulative techniques captured crowds and carried him on an ever full tide of success. In his purposes and methods there was little to differentiate him from a twentieth-century businessman. His assimiliation into contemporary culture all but complete, he was indeed the Christ of culture.

Public response to this strange portrait is attested by the phenomenal circulation—three fourths of a million copies—which the book achieved a generation ago. But this celebration of a Christianity which conforms to contemporary attitudes and reinforces them is far from exceptional. Schneider and Dornbusch were able to bring into a coherent picture forty-six best sellers, of which the Barton book is one, in the "inspirational religious literature" of the period 1875-1955. Although they noted exceptions in works such as those of Harry Emerson Fosdick and Elton Trueblood, they found certain constant elements running through most of this "Popular Religion" literature. To some of them no thoughtful believer would take exception: the promise of a clarification of meaning in life, the heightening of the sense of individual worth, the discovery of power to live by, and the belief that Christ is divine. About others there is cause for serious question: the promise of ease in making decisions; success and happiness in this world,

---

[15] Indianapolis: Bobbs-Merrill Co., 1925.

not as a possible concomitant of faith but a primary expectation; the gift of health and wealth; the absence of eschatological concern and the near absence of consideration of a God of judgment; a steady pragmatic appeal to the proposition that belief in God is true because it "works"; a conviction that man is inherently good; and a social view limited to interpersonal relationships, almost completely ignoring the need to examine the institutional realities of the political and economic world as matters of concerned responsibility for the Christian.[16]

As a kind of keynote to this approach to religion, a key sentence from Emmet Fox reflects the mood of this literature.

> If only you will find out the thing God intends you to do, and will do it, you will find that all doors will open to you; all obstacles in your path will melt away; you will be acclaimed a brilliant success; you will be most liberally rewarded from the monetary point of view; and you will be gloriously happy.[17]

Not only do such portrayals falsify many of the cardinal insights of biblical faith; the claims of this popular religion contain the dangers of a tendency toward magic. For they propose to leave their devotees at the center of life, not so much surrendered to the divine reality as manipulating it for their own advantage.

This caricature of Christian faith is widely pervasive. Schneider and Dornbusch, indeed, follow Dwight Macdonald in referring to "a Gresham's Law in cultural as well as monetary circulation: bad stuff drives out the good, since it is more easily understood and enjoyed."[18] One must assume its presence among the presuppositions of at least some hearers whenever the gospel is presented. To the extent this is true, it must

---

[16] Louis Schneider and Sanford M. Dornbusch, *Popular Religion: Inspirational Books in America* (Chicago: University of Chicago Press, 1958), p. 38 f.

[17] *Power Through Constructive Thinking* (New York: Harper & Brothers, 1932) as quoted in Schneider and Dornbusch, *ibid.*, p.1.

[18] *Op. cit.*, pp. 140-41.

be taken into account as a factor not advancing the dynamic encounter with Christ but inhibiting it by interposing a falsified figure which obscures the Christ of the New Testament.

IV

The call to preach entails a commission to awaken men to the dangerous errors of this idolatry. Toward a provocative encounter with the gospel note five avenues along which the message can march.

At a first and obvious level, the pseudotherapy of this popular cult should drive the minister to a reexamination of the role of Christian faith in relation to health. The oft-repeated promises to cure bodily ills apart from any real interest in objective examination of the relevant health data demand critical examination. One who undertakes this task will need diligent study of the careful and responsible investigations conducted by Leslie D. Weatherhead,[19] Carroll A. Wise,[20] and others. The claim to offer techniques of mental health through oversimplified affirmation of well-being should call forth a renewed emphasis of the insights of such psychiatrists as Karl Menninger. Unrest of spirit, he points out, is so surely a mark of life that one of the most real pleasures is achieved through the progressive solution of the problems that arise day after day. There is a resistance about the conditions of life which calls forth continuous struggle; and the rhythm of doing battle and periodically seeing some victory won, of daily labor and nightly rest, comprises the real drama of living. Men turn aside from this struggle to pursue a mythical peace of mind at cost of self-delusion. Menninger concludes: "It is the search to which I object, because striving for personal peace means turning one's back on humanity and its suffering, losing one's life in trying to save it." [21] This age needs vigorous preaching

---

[19] *Psychology, Religion, and Healing* (Nashville: Abingdon Press, 1951).
[20] *Religion in Illness and Health* (New York: Harper & Brothers, 1942).
[21] Karl Menninger in *The Churchman*, as quoted in Halford E. Luccock, *Romans and First Corinthians*, Vol. I of *Preaching Values in the Epistles of Paul* (New York: Harper & Row, Publishers, 1959), p. 40.

which points that truer way to mental health and well-being.

At a second level, the social inadequacy of the gospel of accommodation should sound an alarm. In his role as "watchman," the preacher cannot but alert men to dimensions of God's Word which this popular message ignores or suppresses. In 1820 the admission of Missouri to the Union as a slave state wrung from Thomas Jefferson the cry, "Like a fire bell in the night, it awakened and filled me with terror." In a time of worldwide upheaval, in the presence of issues which grow more aggravated the longer they are deferred, and in confrontation with the choice between informed, vigorous action and catastrophe of ultimate proportions, it is treachery to encourage a false sense of well-being.

Yet this popular religion joins with other factors in our common life which provoked Aldous Huxley to characterize us as tranquilized, adjusted, and distracted while we engage in crucial competition with Communist peoples who are stimulated, propagandized, and concentrated. Our society honeycombed with crime, our internal life torn by the strife and deep ferment of racial discrimination, and our continents engulfed in crisis, we are menaced by potential nuclear holocaust. "In such an hour, there is a sense in which peace of mind is not an achievement but an accusation." [22] True encounter with Christ will not so much alleviate concern as awaken and direct it. As he himself said, "Do not think that I have come to bring peace on earth; I have not come to bring peace, but a sword" (Matt. 10:34).

At a third level, one notes that this popular religion is built on a philosophy of life which falsifies the realities that must be faced. It persists in a "be good and you'll be happy" interpretation which events belie, which the biblical drama of Job was written to refute, and which Jesus' call to each disciple to bear his own cross repudiated. During World War II Lewis Mumford quoted a university student's criticism of

[22] Pearson, op. cit., p. 113.

American education which might with equal justice be directed toward superficial religion. She said:

> We have decided that the main trouble with our education is that our parents and teachers fed us with fairy tales; they taught us that we lived in a world where everyone had a right to be happy, and where he would certainly achieve happiness if he managed to get a sufficient income. That kind of philosophy isn't very useful to us now, when we have to say good-bye to our lovers or our husbands whom we have just married and may never see again. We suspect that this fairy tale kind of happiness never was real in the first place; now it seems a cheap five-and-ten-cent-store substitute for something harder and better, harder to get and better worth keeping.[23]

When the encounter with Christ is real, it brings one face to face with a Lord who builds squarely on that harder and better understanding of life, saying: "If any man would come after me, let him deny himself and take up his cross and follow me" (Mark 8:34). No call to deny oneself *things*—like giving up cookies in Lent—this is a demand that one deny precisely *oneself* which a religion promising to "bring you what you want" [24] refuses to obey.

Paul points to a fourth level of inadequacy as he writes: "For the desires of the flesh are against the Spirit, and the desires of the Spirit are against the flesh" (Gal. 5:17). Here "the flesh" does not so much signify the body as the whole complex of world-centered wants, the products of our absorption in the world of here and now. A religious orientation which leaves this inwardly divided *wanter* in the center, his plight only deepened by the assurance that the Spirit of God can be manipulated into complying with his wants and fulfilling them, is in need of the note which popular religion

[23] *Values for Survival* (New York: Harcourt, Brace & World, Inc., 1946), p. 230. Used by permission.
[24] The promise is offered in these words on the dust jacket of William R. Parker and Elaine St. Johns' *Prayer Can Change Your Life* (Englewood Cliffs, N. J.: Prentice-Hall, Inc., 1957).

omits and which the New Testament preaching always included: the call to repentance as a total reorientation of life toward the purposes of God revealed in Jesus Christ. Despite the growth in church attendance and membership during recent years, there can be no real revival of religion until there is a new depth of repentance.

At a fifth level it is important to note that, although it is sometimes said that this Christ of culture religion achieves its popularity because it meets persistent needs of men, the real needs lie at a level which cannot be reached by "positive thinking." We do not so much need new thoughts as a new relationship. A prominent psychotherapist reported that in the decade of the 1930's the ills he most frequently discovered grew out of hostility, in the 1940's they centered in anxiety, more recently they have had their source in alienation. We are a people cut off from our roots, not only by our high mobility but in the deeper sense in which theology speaks of separation as the essential character of sin. Beyond the moral connotation of sin as wrongdoing there is a metaphysical dimension in which every man stands separated from his brother men, from himself, and from God.

Gilbert K. Chesterton spoke profoundly when he said that the good news of the gospel is just the good news of original sin. For this is the news which says: You do not have to continue in your alienated state. The life you now live is not the life for which you were created; there has been a Fall, a profound disturbance of the nature for which you were destined. What we can make of ourselves by manipulation of this fallen, alienated nature is not all that can be made of us. Our isolation is not the final condition. "So we are ambassadors for Christ," says the preacher who calls to the dynamic encounter, "God making his appeal through us. We beseech you on behalf of Christ, be reconciled to God" (II Cor. 5:20).

A theology of relationship can light up the interpretation of the Scriptures and guide preaching toward meeting the human situation at the level of its deepest need.[25] A brief glance at the New Testament parable of the Pharisee and the tax collector (Luke 18:9-14) must suffice as a sample approach. In many a sermon this parable has sparked an appeal to cultivate the virtue of humility. Taking his cue from the closing line—"for every one who exhalts himself will be humbled, but he who humbles himself will be exalted" (18: 14)—the preacher pleads: Be humble, for only so can your life find fulfillment. Such exhortations intensify the familiar quandry of the man whose fellow townsmen gave him a medal for being the humblest man in the community, only to have to withdraw it again because one day he wore it! The parable is far more than a call to the kind of right thinking which cultivates humility as a noble virtue. It is a vivid picture of life in and out of relation to God. We quickly recognize the Pharisee as morally the better man. The clue to his fatal alienation, however, is given in the words, "The Pharisee stood and prayed thus with himself" (18:11). Even in his prayer he was alone! He thought positively about himself but was left in separation as deep as before. His prayer revealed contempt for the tax collector and separated him from his brother. Its adulation of his own virtues betrayed the depth of his separation from realistic self-understanding. Its assumption that his salvation rested on his virtues, quite apart from divine grace, was symptomatic of his separation from God.

The tax collector's salvation lay not in moral virtues, nor positive attitudes, nor skill in using prayer as a means of getting what he wanted, but in a penitent cry for a restored relation: "God, be merciful to me a sinner!" (18:13). Here was no praying "with himself," but an agonized cry for God and his forgiveness. "I tell you," said Jesus, "this man went down to his house justified rather than the other" (18:14). In the

[25] Theodore O. Wedel's The Pulpit Rediscovers Theology (Greenwich, Conn.: The Seabury Press, Inc., 1956) is full of insight for the shaping of the preaching message which finds its central strategy in this idea of relationship.

63

language of the Bible, to be justified "means to be brought into right relations with a person" [26] and is achieved not by human effort but by God's gift through Christ. When the repentant sinner reaches out in faith, the relationship is restored and the alienation healed.

As long as he is confirmed in his supposition that he is "inherently good," and encouraged to get what he wants by techniques of thinking which leave him praying "with himself," every man continues in his separation. "For every one who exalts himself will be humbled" (18:14); the ego-wants central to his life will trip him up, leaving him cut off and inwardly divided. "But he who humbles himself will be exalted" (18:14), for in his penitent recognition of need and his outreach of faith he will be met by One who comes to him in dynamic encounter.

We have defined preaching as a divine-human act in which men in their lostness are summoned to a saving encounter with God's Word through the spoken words of a convinced witness. In our survey of the possible relationships between Christ and culture we have seen that the Word Incarnate meets our common life in ways that surprise us and reveal radical conflict between his standards and ours. In the popular religion which grips the minds of many who hear the gospel we have observed the attempt to reduce or eliminate this encounter by assimilating Christ into society as we have made it. At the point where the contemporary mind seeks to evade the saving encounter by substituting an accommodated Christ, we have noted issues which the preacher is called to join between the Word and this falsified popular image. We must now turn our attention to specific disciplines by which the interpreter of the gospel can make his message an instrument of realistic encounter with the ever-changing minds he is sent to challenge.

[26] N. H. Snaith, "Justification," in Alan Richardson, (ed.), A Theological Word Book of the Bible (New York: The Macmillan Company, 1959).

For Further Study

1. Martin E. Marty's *The New Shape of American Religion* (New York: Harper & Row, Publishers, 1959) gives brilliant documentation to much that this chapter has been saying. H. Richard Niebuhr, *Christ and Culture* (New York: Harper & Row, Publishers, 1951) is foundational to the preacher's basic orientation. Theodore O. Wedel, *The Pulpit Rediscovers Theology* (Greenwich, Conn.: The Seabury Press, Inc., 1956) develops the importance of the concept of relationship for the preacher. Alan Walker, *A New Mind for A New Age* (Nashville: Abingdon Press, 1959) presents a significant contemporary preacher's confrontation with society at its points of tension with the gospel.

2. What has been said in this chapter about popular religion obviously looks in too many directions to be an attempt at a sermon. It offers suggestions for a number of different preaching approaches. Select the one most relevant to the needs you sense among your people, relate it to an appropriate text by double analysis, and develop a sermon—bearing in mind that real preaching goes beyond critical analysis to a lifting declaration of God's good news.

4
when we challenge an axiom

How can the gospel interpreter establish contact with the mind he seeks to reach? James E. Sellers has sharpened our thinking on this problem by his contention that when the point of contact is discovered it is generally at some point of conflict. Among second-century pioneers of Christian apologetics he finds Justin Martyr a better guide than Tertullian because Justin did not appeal to the Greek philosophers as incipient Christians. Rather he saw them as teachers of half-truths which led not so much to knowledge as to error.[1] In his appeals to philosophy, Justin did not seek to establish the credibility of the gospel by finding common ground, but only to "communicate with his hearers in their own peculiar symbols." Such intimations of truth as the philosophers possess become full knowledge, Justin declared, only when they are illumined by the light that comes from Christ.

Justin's example can guide the contemporary interpreter in reaching today's "outsider." Nurtured in a culture on which Christian influences have long exerted formative pressures, even the non-Christian man of good will is actuated by value systems which stem from Christian roots. To present the gospel by appeal to a point of contact which places the Christian stamp on these values is to encourage the outsider in the illusion that he is already partly Christian and Christian at the points that seem to him to matter most. Continuing in his alienation from God, unsurrendered and attempting to build a life around his sovereign ego, he is left an outsider still, only the more deeply confirmed in his contentment with

[1] James E. Sellers, The Outsider and the Word of God (Nashville: Abingdon Press, 1961), p. 64.

his present state. William Temple illustrated this predicament during World War II when, speaking of a presumably Christian British society, he said:

For at least half a century its predominant culture has been what is called Humanism, which consists, roughly speaking, in the acceptance of many Christian standards of life with a rejection or neglect of the only sources of power to attain to them. The result was a decline from those standards in all respects in which conformity to them involved serious self-discipline.[2]

Membership in the Christian community does not free a man from the fallibility of his creaturehood or from his liability to sin. The "insider" is always to some degree an "outsider" from the gospel's way of looking at life. Having affirmed the Christian faith, he easily assumes that his ideas are now Christian ideas, his purposes Christian purposes. The problem of interpreting the gospel to him becomes in no small degree the problem of helping him to see how God still addresses him as one called to repentance and to a growth in grace which, in widening areas of his thought and life, requires radical change. To preach effectively to the insider, no less than the outsider, is thus to challenge his axioms.

The dynamic idea which underlies the sermon must of necessity express some form of this tension. The preacher himself stands among those addressed by the Word; and if he has heard it truly, his own ideas and attitudes will come under challenge as he formulates the core of his message. When deeply understood, the Bible speaks in terms of life situations so like our own that the key to incisive interpretation of the text generally lies in the discovery of the point of its challenge to the men of its own time and of ours. Because preachers have been less than realistic in searching out this

[2] *The Hope of a New World* (New York: The Macmillan Company, 1942), p. 64.

basic confrontation, the suspicion has spread that the theological disciplines are a safe refuge from the hard thinking involved in other areas. The suspicion gives point to such caricatures as the popular limerick:

> There was a formidable student in Trinity
> Who solved the square root of infinity.
> But it gave him such fidgets
> To count up the digits
> That he chucked math and took up divinity.[3]

Only a "divinity" so oversimplified as to be rendered false can offer such a haven!

Accuracy in discovering and stating the point of conflict between the gospel and the cherished assumptions of the contemporary mind is crucial in giving effective focus to the ideas from which sermons come. The disciplines this process requires supply essential keys to preaching power.

II

The preacher who most persuades the mind first narrows his subject. And this is best done by bringing some aspect of the gospel into such contact with a need it fulfills, or an idea it contradicts, that the two speak to each other. "Love" is a key word of the Bible and a central reality of Christian experience; yet it is not an adequate preaching subject. No sermon can take unified and purposeful direction from a theme so broad. To qualify it with an adjective, "Christian love," helps little. There are still no boundaries to define meaning. Even to speak of "God's love" does not solve the problem since a subject so stated brings into view only one of the two poles of the dynamic encounter. But bring human sinfulness or human love that seeks to possess into contact with God's love

---

[3] Bennett Cerf, Out on a Limerick (New York: Harper & Row, Publishers, 1960), p. 99. Used by permission.

revealed in Christ, and a preaching theme comes in view. So Oswald C. J. Hoffmann, preaching on "Love That Gives," brings our need and God's answer together to derive his proposition that God's love caused Christ's crucifixion; in response our awakened love enables us to live the crucified life today.[4]

Preaching shares with the arts in the struggle to define its theme. Irving Stone describes Michelangelo's wrestle with this artistic necessity as he prepared to do one of his first important sculptures. At first he knew only that he wanted to interpret worthily the significance he saw in his patron Lorenzo. His mind kept reverting to Lorenzo's observation that in the Greek legend of Hercules the twelve labors were not to be understood literally; they were rather symbols of the gigantic and forbidding tasks confronting each new generation. Little by little his plan formed itself, to celebrate Lorenzo's spirit by heroic portrayal of Hercules. This was only the beginning of the conception, however, for it was still necessary to define and narrow what the statue would say of the mythical hero.

He asked himself questions, for his final result would depend on the ever widening and deepening circles of questions asked and answered. How old was Hercules at the moment of emerging from the marble? Were all twelve of the labors behind him, or was he halfway on his journey? Was he wearing the token of his triumph, the Nemean lion skin, or was he naked to the world? Would he have a sense of grandeur at how much he had been able to accomplish as a half god, or a sense of fatality that as a half human he would die poisoned by the blood of the centaur Nessus? [5]

Before Michelangelo set chisel to stone, it was necessary for him to answer these and a host of other questions which set boundaries around the general subject—Lorenzo—and the

[4] *Op. cit.*, pp. 30-37.

[5] From *The Agony and the Ecstacy* by Irving Stone. Copyright © 1961 by Doubleday & Company, Inc. Reprinted by permission of the publisher. P. 176.

partly narrowed subject—Lorenzo interpreted through Hercules.

In preaching the insight that the point of contact is a point of conflict provides a basic means of meeting this artistic requirement of a subject sharply narrowed and defined. Peter, preaching at Pentecost, found an initial point of contact in a reinterpretation of the excited behavior of the Christian company about which the bystanders had leaped to a mistaken conclusion. "These men," he began, "are not drunk, as you suppose" (Acts 2:15). His presentation of the message of Jesus was not confined to a narration of objective facts, but was rather offered as an event in which his hearers were involved and in conflict with him. "This Jesus," he said, "you crucified and killed by the hands of lawless men" (Acts 2:23). Reinterpreting the words of the prophets in the light of these facts, he produced an effect startlingly at odds with the meanings held by his listeners. From beginning to end he challenged the familiar axioms of their minds until his final demand— "Repent, and be baptized every one of you in the name of Jesus Christ for the forgiveness of your sins" (Acts 2:38)— was in full accord with the major direction the message had established in all its previous steps. In like tension Stephen reinterpreted the history of Israel (Acts 7:2-53); so Paul confronted the Jewish faith in his sermon at Antioch (Acts 13:13-41) and the religious ideas of Greece in his address at Athens (Acts 17:22-31).

Preaching, like teaching, must meet the learner where he is, making contact with his mind through symbols and ideas already familiar to him. In addition to the necessities laid upon teaching and the arts, preaching confronts the additional requirement, growing out of its own essential nature as dynamic encounter with the "otherness" of God, that it meet the listener not to confirm him in his present ways so much as to challenge him at the motivating center of his thought and life. Thus the narrowing of the subject and the work of defining what the sermon will predicate about it must depend

on the degree of accuracy with which the preacher locates the
lostness of those to whom he speaks.[6]

III

One of the commissions of the World Council of
Churches, in its studies of Christian evangelism preparatory
to the Amsterdam Assembly, initiated studies of what they
called "axioms of the modern man." The venture can illumi-
nate how preaching is sharpened by discovering the point of
conflict. The endeavor began when Emil Brunner pointed
out to the study section "that man's thinking is to a considerable extent determined by inner convictions not consciously
thought out or clearly expressed, taking the form of Axioms
of contemporary proverbial wisdom." [7] A complicating factor,
he continued, lay in the fact that most of these axioms are at
odds with "the general structure of biblical thought and
ideas."

Various national delegations pursuing this lead attempted
to crystallize the axioms most commonly taken for granted by
great numbers of their countrymen. What resulted amounted
to a startling delineation of the state of mind to which the
Christian message must be addressed. Almost item by item
the statements are plausible half-truths which call in question
some affirmation important to Christian faith. There is a
strikingly familiar picture of the American mind, not only outside the church but within it, in the "Axioms from America."

[6] It is worthy of note that the confrontation of opposing viewpoints has a
creative significance beyond the immediacies of the preaching situation. It is
in encounter with disbelief or erroneous interpretation that theology itself is
born and continually renews itself. The religious community begins with a
faith intuitively grasped and consisting of attitudes not consciously examined
in the light of intellectual criticism. Only when it finds itself threatened by
conflicting or deviant ideas does it engage in the careful rationalization of its
convictions which then becomes its theological treasure. Cf. Langdon Gilkey,
Maker of Heaven and Earth (Garden City, New York: Doubleday & Company, Inc., 1959), p. 47.

[7] *The Church's Witness to God's Design, op. cit.,* p. 80. An ecumenical
study prepared under the auspices of the World Council of Churches.

1. Truth is established only by proof, and ultimate truth is unknowable.
2. Look out for number one. If you don't, nobody else will.
3. Human nature is fundamentally sound, but needs guidance and correction to achieve its fulfilment. "Sin" is just another name for ignorance and correctible imperfection, or biological lag.
4. There is progress in history, but society may yet destroy itself if the discoveries of science are not controlled.
5. There always have been wars and there always will be. You can't change human nature.
6. "God" is really a projection of man's ideals.
7. A man's religion is his own business and every man has a right to his own belief.
8. Other-worldliness is dangerous because it distracts attention from the effort to gain freedom, security, and justice in this life; and anyway we know nothing about what happens after death.
9. Jesus was a good man. What we need are a lot more people like Him. Now, take Lincoln . . .
10. Do a good turn when you can—but don't be a sucker.[8]

These axioms might well go into the preacher's notebook, each being the kernel of a memorandum from which a sermon will grow after much thought and study. Such a sermon starter should include a scripture passage to provide the basic insight and a vivid statement of some contemporary hunger which it answers or some current attitude it calls in question. Out of the encounter between the Scripture and the need—of which one or another of the axioms may be a pointed expression—a narrrowed subject should be formulated, followed by a paragraph or two in which the possible beginnings of a message are briefly sketched. The notebook in which the preacher works out such seeds for sermons is one of the tools most essential to his craft. By way of illustration, a few pages

[8] *Ibid.*, p. 82.

from such a notebook based on the axioms formulated by Emil Brunner are given in the Appendix to this book.

IV

The axioms formulated at Amsterdam are vigorously provocative and well designed to locate the point of conflict from which the dynamic encounter can begin; yet they need to be supplemented by the preacher's own reading of the assumptions of his contemporaries. Times change. Minds come under the spell of new axioms. In other geographic areas differing axioms prevail. "It is believed," said the World Council commission, "that this method of study can be very profitable, and that others may find it a useful exercise to draw up similar lists of Axioms representing the mind of those groups with which they are most closely in touch." [9] The minister must make his own search for the axioms of his people.

One method of keeping abreast of the developing attitudes of the time is to study the mass media, not for what they say but for their reflection of the things taken for granted concerning their listeners or readers. Such studies find their rationale in what one distinguished journalist calls the "personalities" of respective papers. T. S. Matthews made a study of the editions of the London *Daily Mirror* and the *Manchester Guardian* of the same date, to discover the discrepancies and overlappings in the coverage of what was presumably the same grist of news. The two papers printed a total of 144 news stories of which only 9 were shared in common, 23 appeared only in the *Mirror*, and 71 only in the *Guardian*. The reason for such wide deviation in reporting he attributed to the fact that each selected the news that would fit its "personality" and then wrote it in such a way as to make the fit even more complete.[10]

What is significant for the preacher searching for axioms of the contemporary mind is that papers tend to attract their

[9] *Ibid.,* p. 80.
[10] Thomas S. Matthews, *The Sugar Pill* (New York: Simon and Schuster, Inc., 1959), pp. 17-19.

reading audience from among those who find their "person-alities" congenial. The journal that speaks to a nationwide mass audience which it has won in the intense competition that drives many papers and magazines to the wall may be presumed to have shaped its "personality" in such fashion as to find comfortable acceptance by its vast company of readers. If one can read not only what it says but what it takes for granted, not only its reports but what it regards as worth reporting, not only its facts but its implications, he may arrive at a reflection of its basic assumptions about its readers—assumptions on which it has gambled and won its considerable following.

In the United States the news magazine can tell the story on a nationwide basis better than the daily paper. America has no newspaper of national readership comparable to the Mirror and the Guardian in England. The New York News has a cir-culation approaching 2,000,000, but is mostly sectional in its sales. The New York Times, read more widely over the nation, has only approximately 745,000 daily circulation. Among the news magazines, however, Life surpassing 6,000,000 and Time with well over 2,000,000 are read in every city, village, and hamlet and at every crossroads in the country. Look ex-ceeds Time in circulation, but is similar in character to Life, yet less widely read. Reader's Digest and TV Guide outrank these periodicals in circulation, but since they are not devoted to news reporting, they do not lend themselves to the same kind of study.

For a number of years, classes in Garrett Theological Seminary have periodically searched for the axioms underlying both the reporting of the news and the appeals of the advertis-ing in Life and Time with interesting results. For the news columns they have listed the stories and tried to be sensitive to the implications of any "slanting" they detected, using as a control the summary of the week's news from the Sunday edition of the New York Times for the same period; noting carefully what stories—and particularly what kind of stories

—were selected for inclusion or omission; and asking constantly: What interests and presuppositions does this magazine address in its readers? They have also listed the advertisements of half-page spread or more, noting the commodities advertised and the buyer motives to which appeal was made. Their studies in recent months yielded the following composite list of axioms:

1. It's the *surroundings* that give life its meaning.
2. Religion's all right in its place, but that isn't in politics.
3. Immortality is just your influence going on in the world.
4. These days you have to become a martyr to make the Christian religion real—and I don't have a martyr complex.
5. We must do what's right—to keep other people on our side.
6. You deserve the best; you owe yourself easy-chair comfort. Forget the discomforts of others and live it up. Take care of number one.
7. Is it right? We'll take a vote and see.
8. Certainly we need it; they have one next door.
9. What's new must be good, what's old can't be.
10. Who is God, that we are mindful of him?

The mutual challenge between these axioms and the gospel can help pinpoint areas of conflict significant in presenting the message. The preacher who will hold himself to his own periodic search for the reflection of the current mind mirrored in such media will find in it guidance that will help him locate the lostness of men and speak to his people where they are.

V

Discovering that the point of contact is often a point of conflict, the minister needs clear guiding principles in speaking on matters that put him sharply at issue with his hearers. Difference does not always mean controversy, but it is a tragic day for the church when the note of warning or dissent in its pulpit is silenced or allowed to lapse. With what power that note rings out in the message of the prophets! Hear it in Hosea:

> Hear the word of the Lord, O people
> of Israel;
> for the Lord has a controversy with
> the inhabitants of the land.
> There is no faithfulness or kindness,
> and no knowledge of God in the
> land;
> there is swearing, lying, killing, steal-
> ing, and committing adultery;
> they break all bounds and murder
> follows murder.
>
> —Hos. 4:1-2

While there is evil among a people defiant of God's will, there is no escape from controversy for his spokesmen. So Micah declares:

> Hear, you mountains, the controversy of the Lord,
> and you enduring foundations of the earth;
> for the Lord has a controversy with his people,
> and he will contend with Israel.
>
> —Mic. 6:2

About the risk involved in speaking out on unsettled issues Robert Louis Stevenson said the pertinent word: "For God's sake, give me a young man who has brains enough to be a fool." For fool he may appear if subsequent events prove him to have misjudged the issue. But wrong he is, regardless of events, if he leaves the word of conscience unspoken. As Bishop William C. Martin aptly said, "Christian evangelism that is worthy of the name will not attempt to by-pass issues of a controversial nature. Preaching that avoids this area of life is confined to the marginal and the irrelevant." [11]

[11] News report of an address to the Methodist Council of Evangelism, October 14-20, 1959.

One of the notable prophetic voices of the first half of the twentieth century was that of Ernest Fremont Tittle, who stood ever at the forefront of social advance and helped to shape the mind of the church at large. For more than a quarter century he preached to the same congregation, often sharply at issue with many of his people yet maintaining a bond of love and influence with them. The principles which charted his course distil such wisdom that they may be used as guides through the labyrinth of difficulties in this vital matter.[12]

First, he said, "Always speak from a religious standpoint. Take a text." This initial advise is basic to all preaching; it is never easier to forget, nor more important to remember, than in the heat of controversy. Men listen to a preacher neither for his personal brilliance nor for his expertness in economics, politics, or sociology. His charter for speaking is his ability to interpret the Christian message. There he is on home ground. There he fulfills his function, speaking by leave of no man. Fidelity to his commission should hold him to this center when he speaks on issues under dispute. And his message will be received more readily when he takes his stand on biblical doctrine and from the vantage point of a strong text. Dorothy Canfield Fisher once recalled the action of a Vermont judge who in 1812 refused to order the return of an escaped slave unless the complainant presented "a bill of sale by Almighty God." That took the issue back where it belonged, to its theological premise. There the preacher, of all men, must constantly trace it.

Second, Tittle counseled, "Put yourself in the place of the opposition." Both the Christian ethic and a wise strategy of debate call for looking at disputed matters from the opponent's

[12] Tittle published nothing systematic on controversial preaching, but he spoke on it from time to time in his lectures to ministerial students at Garrett Theological Seminary. Among his papers he left a single page of notes consisting of less than a dozen sentences comprising the seven statements of principle which supply the topic sentences quoted in the ensuing paragraphs. I am indebted to my colleague, John Capps Irwin, for drawing my attention to Dr. Tittle's notes and for his own helpful reflections about them.

point of view. Slanted a little in the restatement, the rival argument is easier to answer—and less worth answering! Refute something weaker than your adversary's keenest statement of his case, and he will say: "Of course you can disprove *that*. But no sane man believes *that*; certainly I do not." The immensely more difficult answer to the argument fairly and strongly stated, however, may carry conviction. Even when the mind is not convinced, the personal bond of understanding between preacher and listener can remain unbroken.

"Praise more often than blame," said Tittle's third maxim. "Be affirmative." The prophetic preacher need not be a scold. Ministers often err by assuming that men know more than they do about the backgrounds of questions and by underestimating their desire to do right. If we instructed them in the faith more consistently and gave them an encouraging word of appreciation more often, there would be less need to apply the lash of exhortation.[18] A congregation soundly instructed in Christian doctrine and viewpoint, and whose minister speaks the lifting word of commendation when he can, will hear him with greater capacity to understand when he feels compelled to take a controversial position.

Tittle's fourth principle stands near the heart of his moving influence: "Speak the truth in love." The church at large knew him as a prophetic preacher; his people revered him as a loving pastor. His ministry to the sick and troubled was notable, and he gave himself unsparingly in it, shirking no call where a ministry to the forlorn required climbing the stairs of a walk-up apartment house, even after his doctor had decreed that his heart could no longer stand the strain. The pastoral root of his prophetic power is revealed in a typical conversation between two conservative laymen after a sermon in which he had taken an advanced position on an aggravated issue. "What did you think of *that?*" asked one man grimly. "Well," the other replied, "I don't see it the way he does—

[18] Cf. John M. Krumm, *Modern Heresies* (Greenwich, Conn.: The Seabury Press, Inc., 1960), p. 139.

yet. But I remember that when my wife was hovering between life and death he sat up all night with me. I believe his *heart* in the matter so much that I'm going to try to understand his mind."

Fifth, Tittle offered a "don't." "Don't offer opinions if you don't have the facts to back them up, or in areas where you have no technical knowledge." This does not excuse the preacher from speaking on matters of conscience; it does demand that he be a diligent and thorough student. If a layman detects errors in fact in the presentation of the case, he cannot be blamed for distrusting the conclusions drawn. The minister who speaks out of thorough knowledge will be heard with steadily increasing respect.

"Give attention to the matter of timing," said Tittle in his sixth point. "You may put it off too long. On the other hand Christmas Sunday is not the time to preach on temperance!" The minister who follows a balanced plan for his preaching and is guided by the rhythm of the Christian year will be greatly aided in his timing. Under the duress of an emergent issue he may be impelled to deviate from his plan occasionally, but he will not as easily go wrong as does the minister whose preaching starts new every week.

Last of his guides for controversy was Tittle's counsel, "Familiarize yourself with recent church pronouncements on controversial issues." Quoting the strong position of one's denomination or of an ecumenical body will make it clear that the minister speaks for the church at large. Because sincere Christians differ widely in interpreting the Scriptures, a Bible text may leave the basic authority of the message open to the charge that it is based on a misreading of the meaning. When biblical exegesis is supported by a declaration of the denomination or of the National or World Council of Churches, it becomes clear that what is said—far from a whim of the preacher's—represents the responsible conviction of the Christian community.

The minister who follows these maxims will not always

79

carry a convinced constitutency with him. Sometimes his convictions will make him painfully unpopular. Occasionally they may exact a more costly price. But his will have been a fruitful ministry who can say, as did Matthew Arnold of the unpopular causes for which he and his colleagues had struggled:

We have not won our political battles, we have not carried our main points, we have not stopped our adversaries' advance, we have not marched victoriously with the modern world; but we have told silently upon the mind of the country, we have prepared currents of feeling which sap our adversaries' position when it seems gained, we have kept up our own communications with the future.[14]

Before venturing into specific areas where the challenge of the gospel confronts the axioms of the contemporary mind, it is well to retrace the steps which have brought us to this point. In the first four chapters we have considered the preaching function and how it may adequately engage the mind of the hearer. This has entailed study of methods for transforming the passive listener into an active participant in the dialogue of the preaching situation; disciplines which enable the preacher to "listen" sensitively to needs which the gospel addresses; the theological bond which alone can re-unite the severed elements of preaching—authority and communication; the nature of the encounter between the hearer and Christ, the living Word; and something of what happens when, in the course of the encounter, we challenge the axioms of men's everyday wisdom. In the chapters that now lie before us we must turn to certain aspects of today's world which, though not exhaustive of the areas of encounter, are strategic pivot points in the winning of the contemporary mind.

For Further Study

1. James E. Sellers has opened provocative lines of thought in his important book The Outsider and the Word of God (Nashville:

[14] Culture and Anarchy, p. 28, as quoted in Fred Eastman, Men of Power (Nashville: Cokesbury Press, 1938), I, 126-27.

Abingdon Press, 1961) which will repay careful study. On the matter of the narrowed subject and the careful articulation of the germ idea from which the sermon stems, the most significant book to appear in many years is H. Grady Davis' *Design for Preaching* (Philadelphia: Muhlenberg Press, 1958). For further reading in principles to guide the handling of disputed questions, Harold A. Bosley's *Preaching on Controversial Issues* (New York: Harper & Row, Publishers, 1953) is rewarding.

2. No discipline can better serve to sharpen a preacher's discernment of facets of the contemporary mind in tension with the gospel than the habit of drawing up axioms assumed by the mass media. Why not take the current issue of *Life* or *Time* and try it now? To follow the steps described in this chapter (pp. 73-75) will require the investment of some time, but it will afford a firsthand view of today's mind, which will be sharper and more challenging to the preacher than any he can find in books because it is his own, stamped with the vividness of immediate perception.

3. If you are not now keeping a notebook of sermon starters, this would be a good time to begin. Why not set aside an hour a day, and challenge the American axioms (p. 72) one by one? You will find a method of writing sermon starters on p. 72. For some sample pages from such a notebook, see what the appendix does with another set of axioms. When you have worked your way through the American Axioms, you might try those written by students (p. 75). Best of all, when you have completed Exercise 2, you will want to let the axioms you have derived spark their own set of sermon starters.

4. Go over your notebook of sermon starters from time to time; add new insights that come to you; carry further your double analysis of the text; incorporate illustrative material that presents itself in the course of your reading, pastoral work, and personal reflection; finally, let the whole process unfold into the divisions of a sermon outline. Do not be in too great a hurry to see the finished sermon; let it cook slowly on the back of the stove! One of these days, however, it will be so nearly ready that you will take it up and do the intensive work that brings it into final form with the joy expressed in the old maxim: "Let not the pulpit drive you to the text, but the text drive you to the pulpit."

part two ———————————
the gospel and today's mind

5

faith confronts the secular mind

"Demas, in love with this present world, has deserted me."
(II Tim. 4:10.) That final lament over a once promising disciple testifies to the inroads of secularism against faith in Christianity's first age. For the swift phrase, "in love with this present world," supplies an almost perfect description of the secularized mind. Derived from the Latin *saecularis*, "belonging to an age," the term "secular" denotes absorption in the affairs and interests of the world of here and now. Over this route the descent of a disciple proceeded from Paul's early commendation, "Demas, and Luke, my fellow workers" (Philem. 24), to his last appearance in the New Testament records, "Demas . . . has deserted me," with its telling explanation—"in love with this present world."

Far from diminished, the attack of secularism has continued to mount so that in our time Georgia Harkness could write a penetrating book substantiating her identification of secularism as "Christianity's major rival in the Western world." [1] Although the contest is sometimes open and explicit, as in the forays of atheism and humanism, it is for the most part the more dangerous because its warfare is undeclared and its avowed goals share common ground with Christian concern for human welfare.

Secularism, in Dr. Harkness's definition, is the organization of life as if there were no God. Recalling John Baillie's remark that we may believe in God "with the top of our minds" or "in the bottom of our hearts," she observes that "most secularists believe in God in the first sense but not in

[1] *The Modern Rival of Christian Faith* (New York and Nashville: Abingdon-Cokebury Press, 1952), p. 11.

the second." [2] Without explicit repudiation of formal creedal faith, the secularist quietly gives his major interest to other concerns, reposing ultimate trust in other forces. The proverbial wisdom of the modern man expresses the secularist mind in axioms from Britain ("There may be a God—but what does it matter?")[3] and from Germany ("It seems as though God plays a part in the lives of certain people. Unfortunately I myself have got beyond this stage!").[4] Neither statement contests God's reality; both dismiss him from consideration as a factor affecting one's destiny.

Evidences of the widespread influence of this attitude are not difficult to find. On the heels of the orbiting of the first Russian sputnik, a song gained currency in East Germany which, in English translation, declared:

> My heart is filled with pride, with reverence and with love for the scientific giants who are opening the door to the universe for all mankind. And together with me, millions of others are hoping that this sublime new star may finally bring to pass that which the Star of Bethlehem promised in vain: peace on earth.[5]

In America the reaction to Sputnik, less ecstatic and given to no denials of the Star of Bethlehem, was characterized by a hysteria which betrayed our dazed fascination with the affairs of this world. The wave of insistence on crash programs of technological training at the cost of the humanities witnessed eloquently to our unspoken confidence in physical as contrasted with spiritual forces. Apart from dramatic world events, a reading of any week's issue of a popular news magazine puts the spectacle of secularism on glamorous parade. The axioms of the contemporary mind derived by students (page 75) constitute a secularist credo with a startling crescendo in the question, "Who is God, that we are mindful of him?"

With this mind preaching finds its point of contact at a

[2] *Ibid.*, p. 11 f.
[3] *The Church's Witness to God's Design, op. cit.*, p. 81.
[4] *Ibid.*, p. 83.
[5] Quoted from Elsa Czech-Kuckhof, in Solberg, *op. cit.*, p. 241.

point of conflict. Demas goes to church each Sunday in considerable number, taking his place in the pews of churchmen and visitors who cherish the "values" Christianity has deposited in the life of our civilization but who have been content, in Elton Trueblood's famous metaphor, to pluck these benefits like cut flowers without comparable concern for their roots in the faith that gave them life. Gospel proclamation must challenge the mind of a generation far removed from our Lord's injunction, "Seek first his kingdom and his righteousness, and all these things shall be yours as well" (Matt. 6:33).

II

One who would speak movingly to the secularist mind must first discern clearly where its consequences lead, for their impact on beheavior is searing. George N. Shuster, marking the secularist's assumption that he can have what he wants without breaking "any 'sensible' code of morals," traces what that entails.

You can assert, for example, that God certainly wants men to love their country; and then you can go on to ignore the manner in which he has decreed that such love should take shape, and end by attributing to the aggressive state any right and power it may claim. Or you may hold that the "essence of religion" is to be honest and courteous, which means being sportsmanlike on the golf course one substitutes for worship every Sunday morning. To take a final example, you may feel that love between the sexes is valid only when the element of physical rapture in it is intense, and so you may end up with seven husbands or seven wives, each presumably a trifle more rapturous than the others. Therewith, without ceasing to be reasonable or even decorous, you have substituted for Christian faith everything which is the opposite of that faith.[6]

[6] "Secularism in the Church," *The Christian Faith and Secularism*, ed. J. Richard Spann (New York and Nashville: Abingdon-Cokesbury Press, 1948), pp. 78-79.

The sense of sin is rationalized away by giving canonical stature to the phrase, "Everybody does it." Faith's conviction that sin is separation from God loses relevance in the secularist assumption that the attractive things of this world are all that really matters. If "everybody does it," it has the ultimate sanction. In his novel, *The Winter of Our Discontent*, John Steinbeck portrays a "respectable" community guided by this maxim. When the teen-age Allen Hawley is proven to have won an essay contest by flagrant plagiarism, for instance, his only emotion is not shame for what he has done but vengeful wrath against the person who brought his dishonesty to light. To his father's attempt to awaken his conscience, his rejoinder is defiant: "Who cares? Everybody does it. . . . Don't you read the papers? Everybody right up to the top." [7]

Steinbeck has constructed his novel on this theme in obvious concern about a society in which moral deterioration has progressed far in allegiance to this relativistic ethic. One sees it in the "white collar crime," with its staggering annual bill of billions of dollars, which Frank Gibney studies in his book *The Operators*. "After all, the reputable-looking Operator would protest, 'Isn't everybody doing it?' " [8] At the other end of the social scale, the figure high in the councils of syndicated crime, whose extended case study fills John Starr's shocking book, *The Purveyor*, justifies his career on exactly the same grounds. "To me," he told Starr,

making alcohol or whiskey without permission from the Government is not what you could call a real crime. . . . Everybody and his brother was either making it or drinking it, but Uncle Sam said both things were against the law. All my life I have been supplying things that people really want that the law says they shouldn't have. They are going to get what they want anyway if I die tomorrow, so why not get it from me? [9]

[7] New York: The Viking Press, Inc., 1961, p. 277.
[8] New York: Harper & Row, Publishers, 1959, p. 4.
[9] *The Purveyor: The Shocking Story of Today's Illicit Liquor Empire* (New York: Holt, Rinehart & Winston, Inc., 1961), pp. 45-46. Used by permission.

J. Edgar Hoover traces both the defections from honesty by the socially acceptable and the brutal exploits of the acknowledged criminal to a common source in secularism. He declares:

The secular notion that whatever gets results is good, the secular preoccupation with goods and gadgets, and the secular indifference to what Paul calls "the unsearchable riches of Christ"— these ultimately find expression in the man who takes a short cut across all the moral and legal codes of humanity and grabs what he wants by force. The difference between this man and the man who, by devious practices, spends his life accumulating wealth, totally indifferent to the moral choas around him, is merely a difference of technique.[10]

An unresolved problem of American education gives this dangerous attitude rootage in our intellectual orientation. The separation of church and state is a doctrine important to the health of democracy and its churches. Yet we have implemented it in an attempt to induct young minds into meaningful life in society without reference to any relation of the affairs of the world to a sovereign God. The resultant "objectivity" assumes that natural phenomena and human relationships can be studied in full segregation from the faith assumptions of either student or teacher. This tradition of assumed objectivity which rules committed loyalties off limits for the intellectually respectable has led to what Howard Lowry calls "the treason of the scholar": "Refusing to be a committed man, he allowed himself to be an uncommitted child. He was ripe for the plucking by any committed brute that came along." [11] Or, as A. C. Craig put it, "The besetting sin of intellectuals is to bite off more than they choose." [12] The gospel confronts the secular mind with a call to radical choosing—"Seek first his kingdom" (Matt. 6:33).

[10] "Secularism—A Breeder of Crime," Spann, op. cit., p. 182.
[11] The Mind's Adventure (Philadelphia: The Westminster Press, 1950), p. 74.
[12] Preaching in a Scientific Age (London: SCM Press, Ltd., 1954), p. 105.

III

Not only does preoccupation with this world erode away the convictions that sustain righteousness—its glorification of the exclusively human paradoxically undermines human dignity. With the goals espoused by the secularist the Christian can have no quarrel. The intent is to serve human welfare, ennoble man, and advance all that is in the best sense humane. For these high objectives secularism has made man an end in himself, taught him that he has only himself to depend on, and held aloft the tenet that man exists in his own right.

Despite its laudable intentions, it has reached disappointing destinations. Coming to flower in the late nineteenth and early twentieth century, this philosophy shaped the mind of the generation that won dubious distinction as the bloodiest in history. Far from dignifying man, it killed 63 million persons and maimed countless millions of others in two world wars, liquidated 6 million Jews, saw the blood purge widely used by both Nazi and Soviet governments against their own people, worked out the techniques of brainwashing, perfected weapons which their inventors declare have power to annihilate civilization, and now lives under conditions of racial injustice in which tensions mount toward catastrophic eruption.

This tragic denouncement is not surprising. For secularized man divorced from relation to any divine reality beyond himself is left as one object among many in a universe shorn of ultimate sanctions. He is made an object of knowledge which the sciences seek to describe with no residue left beyond the reach of their combined disciplines. So, as Paul Tillich concludes: "Man actually has become what controlling knowledge considers him to be, a thing among things, a cog in the dominating machine of production and consumption, a dehumanized object of tyranny or a normalized object of public communications." [13] Thus reduced, he falls lower than other

[13] *Systematic Theology* (2 Vols.; Chicago: University of Chicago Press, 1951), I, 99.

members of the brute creation; for no other animal is en-
dowed with such ingenious capacity to threaten, incon-
venience, and frustrate others of his own species. Sartre stig-
matizes the secularist reduction in his famous line, "Hell is—
other people." [14] H. L. Mencken summed up the human
plight when humanism has gone full circle: "The cosmos is
a gigantic fly-wheel making 10,000 revolutions a minute. Man
is a sick fly taking a ride on it."

The Bible reads man's meaning otherwise. It records a
high identity. The Old Testament declares his origin: "So
God created man in his own image" (Gen. 1:27); and the
New Testament points to his destiny: "Beloved, we are God's
children now; it does not yet appear what we shall be, but
we know that when he appears we shall be like him, for we
shall see him as he is" (I John 3:2). The severance of this
relation has produced desperate lostness. Indeed, as a people
better instructed might have foreseen, this generation has
retraced a familiar course. Beginning with self-glorification—
"Your eyes will be opened, and you will be like God" (Gen.
3:5)—we have arrived at the bitterness of our own lost Eden.

IV

In one of its manifestations secularism wears the garb of
scientism. This pathetic faith makes a cult of the expectation
that the sciences can fulfill the messianic role of man's salvation. Sophisticated minds sometimes give expression to this
faith, as when Aldous Huxley declares, "The advance of
natural science, logic, and psychology has brought us to a stage
at which God is no longer a useful hypothesis . . . a faint trace
of God still broods over the world like the smile of a cosmic
Cheshire cat. But the growth of psychological knowledge will
rub even that from the universe." [15] More frequently it appears among the badly educated who know only wisps and

[14] Jean-Paul Sartre, No Exit and The Flies, English versions by Stuart Gilbert (New York: Alfred A. Knopf, Inc., 1947), p. 61.
[15] As quoted in Lowry, op. cit., p. 32.

patches of science at second hand but who venerate the man in the white coat whose exploits and pronouncements glitter across their TV screens. In lines he called a "Minor Litany," Stephen Vincent Benét gave liturgical expression to the cry for salvation wrung from the hearts of men who have only the cult of scientism to cling to.

> This being a time confused and
>   with few fixed stars,
> Either private or public,
> Out of the darkness I make a litany
> For the lost, for the half lost,
> For the desperate.
>
> Chloral have mercy upon us,
> Luminol have mercy upon us,
> Nembutol have mercy upon us.
>
> Freud have mercy upon us,
> Life have mercy upon us.[16]

Scientism centers in the belief that the methods and procedures which have achieved brilliant success in the physical sciences can be readapted to the development of a science of man in the same exact sense. Proposing no mere methodology for helping man to achieve goals conceived in religious faith, philosophical thinking, or free choice, *scientism is essentially the conviction that the goals themselves can be determined by means of scientific research.* By its own methods science could not produce such a conclusion, for it is a product not of tested knowledge but utopian dreams. Though it pins its hope on science, it is itself a kind of secular eschatology. An East German Communist professor spoke its idiom

---

[16] From *Selected Works of Stephen* Vincent Benét, Holt, Rinehart and Winston, Inc. Copyright, 1940, by Stephen Vincent Benét. Reprinted by permission of Brandt & Brandt, p. 461 ff. For this briefer and slightly revised cutting I am indebted to Luccock, *Romans and First Corinthians*, op. cit., pp. 46-47.

as he proposed to substitute this positive faith for the negations of atheism. "It is possible," he said, "to make it clear to the young people that we believe in humanity . . . and that mankind can achieve everything that is necessary for the development of society. This faith in man is the thing we offer in place of faith in God." [17]

Such devotees of scientism propose that what is sometimes called "human engineering" can reconstruct society and mold man himself in the image of what the "engineers" determine it is his destiny to become. The behavioral sciences are trusted both to establish the goals and provide the means. To date, experience in these areas is not reassuring. Experts of presumably equal competence, confronted by the same data, arrive at divergent conclusions. The employment of scientific specialists by agencies of government makes clear that in the end programs must be determined through policy choices which science alone is not competent to arbitrate. Beyond the question of the *possibility of achieving* the results "human engineering" predicts, another arises: Who are to be the engineers? The universal experience that great power corrupts makes a nightmare of the dream that an intellectual elite might be trusted to establish the goals and control the means by which society and the persons who constitute it are to be reshaped. With the realism born of bitter experience Winston Churchill replied to such a proposal: "I shall be content to be dead when that day arrives."

In its conversation with scientism Christian faith makes three assertions. Note first, it says, that the claim to deal with issues "objectively" without reference to metaphysical presuppositions is impossible to fulfill. John Henry Newman foresaw this dilemma in his declaration that where theology is omitted from the intellectual disciplines it will not leave a vacuum but will be replaced by methods and presuppositions less adequately adapted to cope with the ultimate questions.

[17] Hermann Duncker, as quoted in Solberg, *op. cit.*, p. 244.

To attempt to solve important problems with no metaphysics is actually to deal with them on grounds of naturalistic metaphysics arrived at not by open examination and critical thought, but by default.

Note second, faith admonishes, that scientism commits the fallacy of treating man experimentally as if he were only another aspect of mechanistic nature—and then concluding, beyond its data, that in fact that is what he is. It may be necessary to follow experimental procedures which treat men as if they were only somewhat more complicated animals, but if the experimental data then show only mechanistic and animal responses it must not be forgotten that these were all the method was designed to detect. Human dignity involves responsible choice with its concomitants of possible error, suffering, and growth by acceptance and reconciliation; and a method of study which is not designed to take this into account has already screened out all that is most distinctively human.

Note third, faith concludes, that far from existing as an independent savior in its own right, science is deeply dependent on its cultural heritage from the Judeo-Christian tradition. The sciences arose and first came to flower in societies which derived their intellectual and spiritual climate from the Greek mind and from the faith that arose in Judaism and emerged in Christianity. Science has now developed in Oriental societies nurtured by other faiths and in Communist society saturated with atheistic materialism, but it is not native to these environments. It has been naturalized in them after first attaining its brilliant maturity in societies with a strong taproot of biblical religion.

This is no mere coincidence. Biblical faith has nurtured the interior life of these societies in a threefold outlook without which science could not exist: (a) The conviction that this world is neither to be spurned as in some ethnic faiths; nor regarded as devoid of meaning beyond itself as in materialism; nor understood as a manifestation of God, hiding the divine reality behind a facade of physical phenomena which are themselves mere "accidents" and illusions, as in classic Greek thought. It is rather to be valued as the object of God's creation and redemption, worthy of careful investigation and responsible stewardship. (b) The conviction born of monotheism, that this world is not a congeries of separate and unpredictable forces such as the polytheistic faiths symbolize, but the domain of a Reality that is itself one and dependable. (c) Such integrity in the investigator as will restrain him from shading his facts to favor his hypothesis, an integrity nurtured by a faith which brings the strong motivations of grace to the service of a God of ethical righteousness.

V

In confronting the secularist mind, the preacher is called to stress what secularism denies. And the secularist denial is generally not a blatant atheism so much as the contention that life organized around faith in God makes no crucial difference. To revert to the already quoted axiom from Britain, "There may be a God—but what does it matter?" [18] In face of this challenge there is need for strong preaching on the sovereignty of God as William Temple once asserted it: "When we serve Him in humble loyalty, He reigns; when we serve Him self-assertively, He reigns; when we rebel and seek to withhold our service, He reigns." [19]

A secularist age needs preaching which exalts the providence of God and shows with painstaking care that this doctrine does not demand belief in arbitrary, divine whims which favor God's elect. The preacher will do well to meet the mind of his age at the point of its respect for the uniformities of nature—the "natural law" around which much of our thought is formed. J. Wallace Hamilton has set the key in a sermon on providence, in which he presented natural law as the means

[18] *The Church's Witness to God's Design, op. cit.*, p. 81.
[19] As quoted in Margaret T. Applegarth, *Twelve Baskets Full* (New York: Harper & Row, Publishers, 1957), p. 26.

through which the God of divine order accomplishes his ends. Fittingly symbolic is his story of the youngster who said he was going outdoors to play catch with God, and on being asked how he could do that, replied, "I throw the ball up. God throws it back." Adults dismiss the phenomenon with the impersonal term "gravity"; the lad was not wrong in seeing the natural dependabilities as instruments through which God accomplishes his purpose.[20]

Preaching to the secularist mind calls for a new vitality in the presentation of the claims of stewardship. Secularism is such full immersion of life in the claims and interests of this world that they assume control. Stewardship counters that this world, no end in itself, is only instrumental. In Lynn Harold Hough's graphic phrase, "it is the genius of the material to wear the livery of the spiritual." Far from directing life adequately, this world with its hypnotic demands needs direction. Employed for self-serving ends it becomes evil; dedicated to holy ends it partakes of the nature of the holy. It is not self-sufficient; it is God's world. In a sacramental universe, stewardship is a discipline that saves by putting things to their intended uses and a philosophy that gives meaning to existence.

Deut. 8:7-20, ancient challenge to the secularist's mesmerized occupation with the world around him, would lend itself to the kind of double analysis suggested in Chapter Two. Living surrounded by the opulence of the good earth and by attitudes that plainly say, "My power and the might of my hand have gotten me this wealth" (Deut. 8:17), the secularist forgets a fact which a lawyer is said to have taken as basic in a significant case. Retained by a New York firm to verify the title to a piece of business property in New Orleans, he cleared it to the year 1803. The New York firm was not satisfied, however, and asked him to trace it further. Presently they received a letter which read:

[20] J. Wallace Hamilton, *Who Goes There?: What and Where Is God?* (Westwood, New Jersey: Fleming H. Revell Co., 1958), p. 53.

Gentlemen: Please be advised that in the year 1803 the United States of America acquired the territory of Louisiana from the Republic of France by purchase. The Republic of France in turn acquired title from the Spanish crown by conquest; the Spanish crown obtained it by virtue of the discoveries of one Christopher Columbus, a Genoese sailor who had been authorized to embark by Isabella, Queen of Spain, who obtained sanction from the Pope, the Vicar of Christ, who is the Son and Heir of Almighty God, who made Louisiana.

The earth which sustains our "affluent society" is not of our making. Neither is the stable order within which we work, nor the talents which make productive labors possible, nor the temperament which sustains the will to industry. These all point beyond themselves as if to say: "You shall remember the Lord your God, for it is he who gives you power to get wealth" (Deut. 8:18). Far from matters of course or manifest rights, earth's blessings imply obligation; as a socially minded industrialist declared, "Service is the rent we pay for our space on earth." When a man says *that* with any depth of meaning, he has begun to think sacramentally about life. If it is to continue to motivate him, it must draw sustenance from a deep taproot of faith.

Other passages will occur to the preacher, inviting double analysis in the light of the secularist challenge. This age, in which the secularist mind has reached journey's end in the existentialism of Jean-Paul Sartre and his school, may send the preacher to a re-examination of Ecclesiastes with its keynote, "Vanity of vanities! All is vanity" (Eccl. 1:2). An honest, probing book which seeks to solve the riddle of life on the secularist's grounds by recourse to nature, work, and an earthbound philosophy, Ecclesiastes can arrive over this route only at a reaffirmation of the vanity of all human existence. To find power to sustain meaningful life, however, it is forced at last to a breakthrough into faith: "The end of the matter; all has been heard. Fear God, and keep his commandments; for this is the whole duty of man. For God will bring every deed into judgment, with every secret thing, whether good or evil" (Eccl. 12:13-14). For the modern preacher who will live with its quest, enter into its despair, struggle with what it needs for its completion, this book has much to say to contemporary secularism.

Or what of a double analysis of I Cor. 3:11-13, with its suggestion that, whatever the materials with which we build, every man's work is subject to a test by fire which will determine "what sort of work each one has done"? Helmut Thielicke has observed how alarmingly recurrent in today's literature are such symbols of meaninglessness in our work as Hermann Kasack exemplifies in his novel, *City Beyond the River*.[21] In this story two factories work continuously, one grinding stones to bits and the other rebaking them into wholeness, after which they are shipped to the first to be ground once more in an endless repetition of the process.

Is this more absurd, one asks, than the built-in obsolescence on which much of our industrial prosperity rests? Does it grow out of an age which has lost itself in the round of life wholly taken up with the affairs of this world and has found them increasingly devoid of meaning? Robert Maynard Hutchins neatly describes the modern man's sense of being trapped in an existence which has lost its meaning and is built on assumptions that cannot pass the test of fire. "Our real problems," he says,

are concealed from us by our current remarkable prosperity which results in part from our production of arms, which we do not expect to use, and in part from our new way of getting rich, which is to buy things from one another that we do not want, at prices we cannot pay, on terms we cannot meet, because of advertising we do not believe.[22]

[21] Thielicke, op. cit., p. 97 ff.
[22] As quoted by Albert Terrill Rasmussen, "Stewardship in an Economy of Abundance," in *Stewardship in Contemporary Theology*, ed. T. K. Thompson (New York: Association Press, 1960), p. 242.

Concealed from conscious thought the problem may be, but not from the underlying sense of an existence meant for something more than this. Double analysis of this passage from the Corinthian letter and of the prevailing malaise will drive the preacher to the ringing answer struck out in the eleventh verse: "For no other foundation can anyone lay than that which is laid, which is Jesus Christ."

Preaching can serve a vital function in the remaking of a world far gone in secularism. For it can serve in the reshaping of the mind and the awakening of the heart. In these lie the seeds of the future. Let Bishop G. Bromley Oxnam sum the matter up in his report of a conversation with Louis Fischer shortly after the latter had published his book on *Gandhi and Stalin*. The bishop recalls Fischer's remark that Gandhi, though he used political forces, never put his real trust in legislation. He believed that the individual is the crucial concern—an idea in the mind, a desire in the heart more germinal than an act of a legislature. For "he held that when the millions think in a certain way, or feel in a certain way, action in that way is inevitable." [23] Leading persons to "think in a certain way" and "feel in a certain way," namely that this world and our life in it derive their meaning and worth from God's sovereignty over them, is the task and privilege of the preacher—a task not unrelated to the coming of the day when the kingdom of the world shall become the kingdom of our Lord and of his Christ.

For Further Study

1. For a penetrating analysis of secularism, *The Modern Rival of the Christian Faith*, by Georgia Harkness (New York and Nashville: Abingdon-Cokesbury Press, 1952) is significant in its theological perspective and in the wide horizon it draws around the subject. More concerned with how one approaches the secular mind in preaching, is the symposium edited by J. Richard Spann, *The Christian Faith and Secularism* (New York and Nashville: Abingdon-Cokesbury, 1948).

[23] G. Bromley Oxnam, "Secularism and the Christian Faith," Spann, *op. cit.*, p. 288.

Part of Donald O. Soper's Lyman Beecher lectures of 1960, *The Advocacy of the Gospel* (Nashville: Abingdon Press, 1961) speaks forthrightly on this subject. William Whyte, Jr., of course is discussing matters that run far beyond scientism in *The Organization Man*; nevertheless scientism is subjected to an unusually able critique in that volume.

2. Taking one or more of the approaches to preaching suggested in this chapter, begin to develop a sermon plan for each in your notebook. Be sure to make the message your own by (a) firsthand study of the context and exegesis of the suggested Scripture, checking the best commentaries at your disposal; (b) setting down the names of persons you have dealt with this week, noting the needs to which this sermon should speak; (c) noting axioms of the modern man, either from the lists reported in Chapter Four and the Appendix, or from your own investigation of mass media, that seem to have a bearing on the subject; (d) your own extension of the double analysis in the light of these steps.

In your sermon planning be sure that before you begin to work out the detailed outline you clarify the one central thing the sermon is to say. This central idea should be stated in one straightforward sentence; if you cannot put it in a single sentence the probability is strong that it is not a single unified idea. This central idea or proposition is vital to everything else you do in the preparation and the preaching. Work it out with great care, and then make every section of the sermon clarify or support that one sentence.

6
the gospel and the crisis in character

Looking ahead at the close of World War I, the scholarly and idealistic editor of the *Manchester Guardian* assessed the task of building a humane world society. Only one foundation material could be used he said—personal character; but as a matter of tragic fact, the bricks were running short. The shortage has been so long extended that, amid the thunders of World War II, discerning thinkers identified the world upheaval and the long shadow it cast over the future as still a breakdown in character. In the latter half of this tragic century that crisis is assuming apocalyptic proportions.

Gamal Abdel Nasser of Egypt dramatized our plight when he said of the Arab peoples: "We have come, in almost a single step, from the age of feudalism to the age of the atom." Invested with this ultimate destructive potential, we have shown little capacity for the stewardship demanded in the aphorism, "This must be the best generation—or the last."

The secularization of life has taken a costly toll. Absorbing the human within the world of things, it has reduced man's value to his utility. Material ends his goals, earth-centered forces his final trust, himself a phenomenon to be explained without residue by the "objective" sciences, the individual's worth ends with his usefulness. The Nazi leader who, after a late afternoon amid gracious surroundings listening to the music of Mozart, gave the order which sent innocent men to their death revealed the inherent tendency of life organized on this basis. Required to be the best generation, we have built on principles which evoke the worst.

In this crisis Christian faith is profoundly concerned. Theology has uncovered the futile emptiness of moralism as a message. The gospel is more than a summons to ethical right-eousness. Yet the New Testament rings with the certainty that unless righteousness ensues, God's great invitation has not been truly accepted. Christian proclamation is more than exhortation. Its basic word is no imperative "we must," or "thou shalt not." It is clear that where the moral demand stands alone or dominant it requires of man what alone he cannot fulfill. Deepening his anxiety and despair, it renders salvation impossible. The apostolic message heralds the grace of God, assuring man that though he is a sinner in constant need of repentance he is a *forgiven* sinner. The recovery of this note in the Reformation brought a new springtime to the world. It remains the indispensable gain of the biblical theology of our time.

Yet the word of grace is never solitary. The Reformation gave unequivocal allegiance to God's law. Wherever the in-fluence of Calvin prevailed, men grew certain that their place among the elect could be attested only by such fruits as the Puritan character and such sturdy virtues as forged the link between Calvinism and the rise of capitalism. Luther's the-ology of grace included an emphasis on God's law, understood as far more than the biblical commandments. He held that the Law is so embedded in the structure of the world that the obligations between the magistrate or the father and those dependent on them are a part of the Law as God has ordained it. The Protestant doctrine of vocation arose from this sense of responsibility inherent in our life under God.

From the perspective of biblical theology the Christian message is always incomplete unless the law's demand comes boldly into view. The climactic Pauline message of grace in the eighth chapter of Romans is meaningless unless it is seen as the answer to the desperate struggle with law in Rom. 7. Jesus underscored the call to character as, in Matt. 7:19-23, he repudiated any relation to those whose orthodox faith ("Lord, Lord") or eloquent preaching ("Did we not prophesy in your name?") or useful Christian labors ("and cast out demons in your name, and do many mighty works in your name") were not attested by fruits in character. "Not every one who says to me, 'Lord, Lord,' shall enter the kingdom of heaven, but he who does the will of my Father who is in heaven."

Paul was sure that new life is God's gift in Christ, but this conviction did not diminish his certainty that the Christian who has received the gift is called to show fruits in character. To the Colossians he wrote, "If then you have been raised with Christ, seek the things that are above, where Christ is, seated at the right hand of God" (Col. 3:1). Climactic to his impassioned defense of the freedom of the just who live by faith is his catalogue of the fruits of two ways of life, in the flesh and in the spirit. Seeing the flesh as more than bodily appetites, he wrote of it as life absorbed within secularized culture apart from God:

Now the works of the flesh are plain: immorality, impurity, licentiousness, idolatry, sorcery, enmity, strife, jealousy, anger, self-ishness, dissension, party spirit, envy, drunkenness, carousing, and the like. I warn you, as I warned you before, that those who do such things shall not inherit the kingdom of God.

—Gal. 5:19-21

Though he declared that those led by the Spirit are not under the law (Gal. 5:18), he was clear that these character flaws mark life outside the kingdom. With equal power he portrayed the consequences in character which follow life in the Spirit: "But the fruit of the Spirit is love, joy, peace, patience, kind-ness, goodness, faithfulness, gentleness, self-control; against such there is no law. And those who belong to Christ Jesus have crucified the flesh with its passions and desires." (Gal. 5:22-24.)

To a man or an age not deeply involved in the struggle with the problem of character, the preaching of grace can have little meaning. The hopelessness of the unaided battle to set life right by our own power renders the word of grace and forgiveness matchless good news. But the man who has not given serious concern to the bitter struggle will make little sense of the announcement of a remedy for his frustration. The gospel meets the contemporary mind with the saving word for the crisis in character, but it must first bring the crisis itself into focus.

II

Though this crisis ultimately confronts the solitary individual, it can be seen with initial vividness in the dark tide of crime that rolls across American society. In the most recent year for which government crime reports are available, a murder occurred every hour, a case of forcible rape every thirty-five minutes, a robbery every seven minutes, an aggravated assault every four minutes, an auto theft every two minutes, one larceny of over fifty dollars every minute, and a burglary every forty-six seconds.[1] Shocking in themselves, such figures do not plumb the depths of the crisis in character. Tossed upon the surface of a deeper tide, these violent manifestations indicate the dread power of what rolls beneath.

For a public which frowns on such overt misdeeds responds with bland indifference or tacit approval to other crimes of which these are often the end results. One glaring example exists in what John Starr has called "today's illicit liquor empire." Because illegal liquor, which evades the $10.50 per gallon federal tax, can be sold more cheaply, the American public buys more than 75,000,000 gallons every year. Despite the popular notion that bootlegging arose in the Prohibition era and, save for some minor trickle, stopped with it, Starr's authoritative study sustains the testimony of a successful producer of illegal liquor concerning the prosperity of that business in more recent times. "All in all," he boasted, "our operation was the biggest thing of its kind that ever happened in the United States; it made everything I'd seen in Prohibition

[1] Based on crime statistics reported by the Federal Bureau of Investigation for the year 1959.

look like kids playing for pennies." [2] A business so vast requires a huge volume of customers. Obviously such a trade area must extend beyond the ranks of the known criminals to include a considerable segment of the public. "What the public does not see," Starr writes, "is that this 'innocent' racket provides a safe haven for murderers, extortionists, rapists, dope peddlers, arsonists, thieves—in short, every known type and degree of law breaker." [3] In the social irresponsibility which patronizes an illegal business to satisfy a thirst more cheaply, appears one link between violent crime and the citizen who would be affronted at any suggestion that he is not a loyal member of respectable American society.

The illict liquor empire, however, constitutes only the "number two racket." It is even more shocking to see the relation of the "respectable" citizen to the trade that *rules* the underworld. "Gambling," reports Fred J. Cook in his exhaustive study, "is the heartbeat of organized crime both on a local and a national scale." [4] It provides the capital on which other criminal enterprises carry on their extensive operations. Milton R. Wessel, who headed the Attorney General's Special Group on Organized Crime, concluded that the American public spends $46,500,000,000 annually on all forms of illegal gambling. The magnitude of this figure is incomprehensible until one recalls that not until the President appealed for special appropriations in the light of the Berlin crisis of 1961 had the Federal budget for national defense ever exceeded $46,-000,000,000. Wessel estimated that about $9,000,000,000 of this amount remains each year in the coffers of the underworld—a "take" approximately equal to the total wholesale price of American automobile production.[5] Obviously no such

[2] Starr, *op. cit.*, p. 182.
[3] *Ibid.*, p. ix-x.
[4] *A Two Dollar Bet Means Murder* (New York: The Dial Press, Inc., 1961), p. 22. Cook is quoting here from the presentment of a Brooklyn grand jury study of gambling in 1958.
[5] *Ibid.*, p. 11.

gigantic business could exist without vast nationwide trade.

Its wide spread is indicated by the New York Crime Commission's discovery of bookmakers with interstate ties in towns of less than 5,000 population, and their report that "it was impossible to find a municipality of 10,000 persons without a bookmaking operation." [6] Parallel studies show that what is true of New York could be duplicated broadly across the nation. The gambling empire was not erected on the desperate wagers of the relatively few big gamblers but, as Cook shows, on "the funds of the two dollar bettor and the fifty cent numbers player."[7] It takes a great many of these to aggregate a sum equal to the Federal budget for national defense.

Those who make these "innocent" two dollar bets would be aghast at the suggestion that they provide the lifeblood for a major attack on national decency, yet the force of that charge is sustained by the most careful investigators. Wessel's study showed that fully half of the $9,000,000,000 of gambling money remaining annually in the tills of the underworld "is earmarked for protection money paid to police and politicians." [8] So the two dollar bet corrupts government. The Brooklyn grand jury declared that "if you scratch the professional operator of gambling ventures, you find the narcotics peddler, the loan shark, the dice-game operator, the white slaver, the murderer." [9] The two dollar bettor and the fifty cent numbers player support that! More serious than the direct drain on the economy, the corruption of government, and the partnership with syndicated crime, is the undermining of individual character in the gambler's quest for something for nothing—a quest, it must be repeated, which has assumed nationwide proportions so gigantic that it plainly honeycombs our society.

This appetite for unearned money has been dramatized repeatedly— in rigged TV quiz programs, payola, convictions

[6] *Ibid.*, p. 13.
[7] *Ibid.*, p. 21.
[8] *Ibid.*, p. 11.
[9] *Ibid.*, p. 22.

for price collusion in high places, and similar scandals. Frank Gibney has shown that these instances which focus public attention are but the outcropping of the iceberg. In a single year, his figures show, $5,000,000,000, or approximately one per cent of the national product, changed hands in "kickbacks, pay-offs or bribes"; while the public was bilked of half a billion dollars in home repair frauds, another half billion in worthless checks, a half billion in embezzlements, $100,000,-000 in mail frauds, and several hundreds of millions in worthless stocks. That same public cheated the government to the extent of an estimated $1.5 billion in tax chiseling.[10] Gibney's study deals not only with so-called "white-collar crime" but with "the wide area of legal but immoral sharp practices in business, labor and politics, often severely damaging to society but generally subtle enough to keep just beyond effective range of society's formidable but fixed legal gun positions." [11] Those who engage in these practices he calls "the Operators." His identification of those involved is frighteningly inclusive. "The Operator," he writes,

may be a bigtime juggler of corporations or a smalltime accountant skillfully barbering a friend's income tax. He may be a salesman padding his expense account to meet the payments on his car. He may take bribes or give them, whether the bribing involves a political scandal or a simple shift of business from one wholesaler to another. He may be a partner in a crooked accident-insurance racket, or a prosperous store owner with a weakness for faked markdowns. Or, all too likely, he may be just a decent, God-fearing American who had to put his finger in the till one day and never found the strength to pull it out.[12]

Gibney's carefully documented study led him to two observations which point to responsibility more broadly based

[10] The Operators (New York: Harper & Row, Publishers, 1959), pp. 6-8. Used by permission.
[11] Ibid., p. 4.
[12] Ibid., p. 5.

than even this inclusive roster might suggest. First, the public is cheated of these appalling sums because of the eagerness of the victims "to make a fast buck faster." [13] Second, restraint of these sharp practices by law is rendered difficult, if not impossible, by the lack of public indignation.[14]

Customers for an illegal liquor business large enough to aggregate $1,500,000,000 a year in revenue lost to the government, patrons for a gambling conspiracy whose profits approximate the gross wholesale income of the automobile industry, and "respectable" sharp practices whose unethical billions defy accurate computation—this is a monumental bill of particulars. Yet these are only symptoms that appear on the surface. What lies beneath is irresponsibility and insatiable acquisitiveness so deep and universal as to amount to a staggering national crisis in character.

III

The sources of the crisis can be found at varying degrees of depth. At the first level one encounters the emphasis which our society places on acquisition. As Gibney points out, the advertising industry devotes its mastery of techniques, its growing insight into the mysteries of motivation, and the full weight of its annual $11,000,000,000 of resources to the task of stimulating the public to covet and acquire. It is not surprising, he observes, that so much skilled stimulation makes people greedy or that those whose greed is continually aroused should sometimes cheat.

Our system of awarding status to those who possess, without too closely scrutinizing how the possessions were acquired, provides an atmosphere which facilitates this movement from acquisitiveness to sharp practice. So, too, does our bestowal of prestige on those who "produce," with so little discrimination about the product, that "The head of a distillery, a drive-in theater, or a dog track is a producer" (and so a sharer in the

[13] *Ibid.*, p. 8.
[14] *Ibid.*, p. 19 f.

accolades given to production) but the high school principal or the parish priest is not.[15]

At a second level, the crisis is seen by some of its students as the product of certain easy-going virtues of what Gibney calls "the Genial Society." He names toleration as one of these —meaning by that term not so much the respect for the personality or rights of another, as an unprotesting acceptance of whatever comes, in preference to making a fuss or being disagreeable.[16] Others have discerned a state of social conditioning in which men are "imprisoned in brotherhood"— meaning none of the realistic acceptance of each other in spite of sinfulness and offenses, which Christian faith builds on the conviction that we are children of one Father and disciples redeemed by one Lord, but rather

that contemporary body of thought which makes morally legitimate the pressures of society against the individual. Its major propositions are three: a belief in the group as the source of creativity; a belief in "belongingness" as the ultimate need of the individual; and a belief in the application of science to achieve the belongingness.[17]

We have devoted some attention (in chapter five) to the utopian faith that science can manage both the means and the ends of salvation in a good society; the other two propositions of the above trilogy now require examination. From the gospel's perspective the group holds high significance but can scarcely be regarded as the "source of creativity," an article of faith which does violence to the Christian recognition of the responsibility and potential of the indvidual. And while faith is deeply aware of the individual's need to belong, it cannot

[15] John Kenneth Galbraith, *The Affluent Society* (Boston: Houghton Mifflin Company, 1958), p. 183.

[16] *Op. cit.*, p. 11.

[17] William H. Whyte, Jr., *The Organization Man* (Anchor Books edition; Garden City: Doubleday & Company, Inc., 1957), p. 7.

grant that "belongingness"—in the sense of smooth adjustments to a peer group—is "the *ultimate* need."

These illusory virtues are closely related to the source of the crisis in character proposed at the third level: the loneliness which makes the individual eagerly responsive to what David Riesman has called "other-direction." In his famous simile he likened the controls which shape much of our contemporary character to "social radar," by which the individual sensitively notes the reactions of others to every nuance of his behavior and modifies his course in conformity to their expectations. In the tragic drama, *Death of a Salesman*, Willy Loman affords a striking example of this pattern in his pathetic concern about being liked. As one kind of man might have measured his life's successes by his conquests—military, amorous, or economic—or another might have judged himself by his degree of nobility in measuring up to a fixed code of conduct, Willy Loman justified his years "on the road" with one wistful phrase: "They liked me." Part of his tragic lack of self-understanding ("He never knew who he was!") lay at this point. For Loman was not one integrated, purposeful individual so much as the sum of his responses to a multitude of others to whose potential likings he had struggled to conform.

As a character in a popular novel summed up his own method of meeting life, it amounted to a simple set of directions: "Find out what they're drinking and drink it, find out what they're thinking and think it, find out what they're wanting and want it." Riesman is talking about character so shaped when he observes that today's other-directed child could make little sense of the advice often given those of a former generation to "make good" since, until he has found it out by the responses of his peer-group, he has not the slightest idea what making good means.[18] From the perspective of Christian faith

[18] David Riesman with Nathan Glazer and Reuel Denney, *The Lonely Crowd, A Study of the Changing American Character* (Anchor Books edition, abridged; Garden City: Doubleday & Company, Inc., 1953), p. 66.

such a mode of shaping conduct amounts to a crisis in character best measured by the contrast between this standard and Paul's counsel: "Do not be conformed to this world but be transformed by the renewal of your mind, that you may prove what is the will of God, what is good and acceptable and perfect" (Rom. 12:2).

From the plight of the other-directed it is a short step to the fourth level: the loss of a center of personal existence. Willy Loman does not know who he is because he is nobody in himself—only a kaleidoscopic series of reflections of others —but this is only part of the explanation. He is content to shape himself thus in the image of what "they liked," because he has lost the sense of being related to anything of ultimate significance beyond himself. John Steinbeck portrays a man with a similar inner vacancy in Ethan Allen Hawley, who says of the anxiety born of this inner emptiness and insecurity, "It rots out your guts. I can't think beyond next month's payment on the refrigerator. I hate my job and I'm scared I'll lose it." [19] These characters, who abound in the literature of our time, have no conviction that life has its source, center, and ultimate dependability in God. They cannot hold original opinions or make independent judgments based on firmly held convictions, because they see themselves not in the image of God, but in the image of a peer group. They live "under the dictatorship of the Zeitgeist" in everything "from the prevailing ideology to the prevailing fashion." [20] Secularism, having organized life as if God no longer lived, has taken its ultimate toll.

IV

Preaching that is sensitive to this contemporary loneliness can speak to it with unique power to heal. For into this sense of personal isolation and insecurity it brings God's personal word through the agency of a person. This potential of the pulpit comes to focus in the case of a Chicago working man

[19] Op. cit., p. 13.
[20] Thielicke, op. cit., p. 46.

who was the victim of a pathological fear of contact with other persons. Employed in maintenance work done in a large office building at night, he rarely encountered another person in his working hours. From his job he went daily to the little room where he lived alone, his life thus arranged to assure almost unbroken isolation. His one contact with the world of persons came regularly on Sunday mornings when he went to church, remaining unnoticed in the large congregation by the expedient of arriving late and slipping away quickly at the end of the service. Yet he felt an identity with the preacher whose strong faith and human warmth conveyed to him a feeling of one who cared and with whom he had a bond. Though he never ventured a face to face conversation, this sense of identification served to anchor his tragically withdrawn life through four solitary years.

In ministering to such loneliness, preaching has unique responsibility. The message incorporated in books cannot replace its service as God's personal word conveyed through a person. Mass media attempt to fulfill the role, as Arthur Godfrey's career illustrates. In a long hospitalization early in his career, Godfrey listened constantly to radio programs and noted that entertainers were addressing "Ladies and Gentlemen of the radio audience," attempting to reproduce the relation of an actor on stage to a theater crowd. Godfrey concluded there was no such audience. "There was just one guy or one girl off somewhere listening by themselves." [21] The development of his highly personalized style of communication grew out of that perceptive conclusion. Yet the mass media cannot fully meet this need; they can offer only a voice or an electronic image on a screen. What men need is a person who speaks a personal word from the supreme Person.

In this, as at all points, Jesus stands preeminent. "When he saw the crowds, he had compassion for them, because they were harassed and helpless, like sheep without a shepherd."

[21] Malcolm Boyd, *Crisis in Communication* (Garden City: Doubleday & Company, Inc., 1957), p. 110.

(Matt. 9:36). The shepherdless sheep is the gospel figure of this desperate isolation and insecurity with a terrifying vacancy at its center. Jesus knew how vulnerable such lonely people could be to temptation, to the blandishments of the demagogue, and to ultimate despair. So he had compassion, a veritable pain of love.[22] In such empathy preaching fulfills its opportunity to serve "the lonely crowd."

One who speaks with understanding can say things to men from the pulpit which can rarely be said in private conversation. Here the ultimate issues and the most personal decisions form the expected content of discourse; matters more trivial are an impertinence. The preacher who understands his role knows that he speaks to men who are alone. Every man is alone with his guilt, and the terror of it lies in the certainty of the guilty soul that no other can share unworthiness like his. Men are alone with feelings of inferiority which separate them from the seemingly assured people they see around them. Each man is alone with the momentous decision to be made in the face of temptation, alone in the agony of his grief, alone in facing responsibility, alone in death. It is always to one man alone before God that the demands of the law and the release of the gospel come. Preaching which understands this solitariness can speak to it without violating the dignity inherent in it.

V

So fully does the gospel enter into dialogue with the crisis in character, and at so many points, that in concluding this discussion we need only lift up three suggestive examples.

It can appeal, first, to explicit decision in the face of the challenges of widespread irresponsibility and other-direction. Courageous resistance to pressures to conform is a treasured tradition of the Christian heritage. Peter and the other apostles

---

[22] George A. Buttrick's exposition of this passage in The Interpreter's Bible (Nashville: Abingdon Press, 1951), VII, 360-61.

spoke in its heroic tone when in the face of threatened penalties for their witness they replied, "We must obey God rather than men" (Acts 5:29). Christians in Communist lands now resist pressures few American Christians have ever known. In East Germany the onslaught against a family in which a young person remains true to the church and its program of confirmation in preference to the Communist Youth Dedication with its indoctrination and materialist pledge of allegiance involves threats to the youth that he will be excluded from school and employment, threats to the father that he will be denied promotions in his work, pressures upon the mother from the women's organizations of the community, appeals to the young person in terms of family loyalty: "Are you going to ruin not only your own life but also the work and the living of your father and mother?" In the face of such pressures the German bishops issued a call to courageous decision, read in pulpits throughout East Germany. "Our answer," they said,

must be that we take Confirmation instruction much more seriously than ever and that together with our children we remain unyieldingly faithful to God and to the Church of Jesus Christ.

Threats should not frighten us. In the years of the great Church struggles we have constantly experienced that God supports His own through all sorts of tribulations. He will not leave us without His help.

It is written, "You should obey God rather than man." And our Saviour Jesus Christ says, "Whoever confesses me before men, him will I also confess before my Father which is in heaven." [23]

Such resistance not only requires strength; it develops it, as Ibsen demonstrates in his portrayal of the heroic Dr. Stockmann in his play, *An Enemy of the People.* Having persisted in his protest against public facilities which carry germs of infection, the doctor has been made the victim of a campaign of vilification which culminates in mob action against him. Gath-

[23] Solberg, *op. cit.*, p. 243-44.

ering the stones that have been hurled through his windows, he declares that he will treasure them and pass them on to his sons as heirlooms. To his wife's fear that he will be driven out of the country, he replies: "Are you out of your mind, Katherine? Drive me out! Now—when I am the strongest man in the town!" "The strongest," she asks, "—now?" "Yes," he replies, "and I will go so far as to say that now I am the strongest man in the whole world. . . . You mustn't say anything about it yet; but I have made a great discovery. . . . The strongest man in the world is he who stands most alone." [24] Jeremiah spoke in the accents of that discovery: "I sat alone, because thy hand was upon me" (Jer. 15:17). There is power in the solitary stand of one man sustained by a God-given conviction.

Preaching can make a second appeal—to the power that comes from living in the light of an invisible environment. Jesus spoke of this resource as he said to the disciples: "I have food to eat of which you do not know." Perplexed, they speculated, "Has any one brought him food?" But he answered them, "My food is to do the will of him who sent me, and to accomplish his work" (John 4:32-34). This was the open secret of his life. Against a hostile environment he had power to go his way through the constant cultivation of purposes stimulated and nurtured by companionship with the unseen. It provided another environment, by far the more influential in determining his course.

Paul lived in the light of such unseen companionship. Whether written by his own hand or by another in his name, the Second Letter to Timothy contains authentic accents of his message. What loneliness could be more crushing than the picture he draws of a man standing friendless before a Roman court? "At my first defense no one took my part; all deserted me." He who had been all things to all men that he might save some, was left without even a character witness to

[24] Henrik Ibsen, Act V. Quoted from *Four Plays* (New York: University Library Publications), p. 113.

say a word in his behalf! "But," he adds, remembering how wonderfully he was sustained, "But the Lord stood by me and gave me strength" (II Tim. 4:16-17). So he was not alone! The gospel message of an invisible environment, an unseen Companion, can bring men to commitment beyond the horizon any "social radar" can scan.

Preaching can appeal, finally, to a great conception of the Church in the light of which men discover that they are less alone. When a woman hurled herself from the eleventh floor of a Chicago office building, leaving behind a suicide note with the single explanation, "I'm so alone," the picture that came to light was sadly typical of modern urban life. She lived in solitude and dull routine: work as a machine operator, the emptiness of her room, an occasional dinner with a few casual associates, the movies, and mass on Sundays. A coroner's juror summed up the comment of sympathetic observers: "She was past her prime. She was alone. What else could she do?"

Perhaps nothing as matters stood. But one who has known the deep sense of belonging that comes with life in the Christian fellowship cannot but yearn to have such lonely souls discover its treasure. Of it Jesus said: "I am the vine, you are the branches. He who abides in me, and I in him, he it is that bears much fruit" (John 15:5). The reference is not to a solitary believer in mystical relation to an unseen Christ. The figure of the vine, familiar to those to whom these words were first addressed, had been the well-worn prophetic image of Israel. It was corporate. It spoke of life within the tightly bound community of the people of God. In Jesus the vine comes to new life. He is not merely the root or the trunk. He is the vine, and one who belongs to him belongs to a wonderful fellowship of shared life. "Lo, I am with you always, to the close of the age" (Matt. 28:20)—that is his personal word to those who share the mission of the fellowship. "If one member suffers, all suffer together; if one member is honored, all

116

rejoice together" (I Cor. 12:26)—that is the nature of the shared life within the fellowship gathered around him.

Jesus spoke a telling word concerning the power of this fellowship to create character. Coming into it, he said, could make a simple Christian tower above even the heroic stature of John the Baptist. "I tell you, among those born of women none is greater than John; yet he who is least in the kingdom of God is greater than he" (Luke 7:28). John's power was that of one man who stood alone—"I am the voice of one crying in the wilderness" (John 1:23). In contrast to this, the power of the simplest Christian is multiplied by belonging to a community of concern, a saving society.

In it men have fellowship not only with the company visible around them, but with a vast host of those who have gone before, into whose trials and triumphs they enter and on whose strength they draw. Despite its overtones of carnage, there is suggestiveness in the scene following the Battle of Fredericksburg depicted by John J. Pullen in his historical study, The Twentieth Maine. At Fredericksburg the regiment, which was to become one of the great units of the Union Army, drew its first fire as a raw, undisciplined mass of recruits —and its losses were heavy. Pullen records how they buried their dead, and then suggests that on this field, where they had been sheltered by the dead, they found their sense of obligation. During the ensuing months of battle the roster of the living decreased and the roll of the dead grew longer, but together the living and the dead were "parts of whatever it was that made up the consciousness of the regiment." [25]

How truly a parallel picture, etched on the memory of time, portrays the Christian fellowship:

Therefore, since we are surrounded by so great a cloud of witnesses, let us also lay aside every weight, and sin which clings so closely, and let us run with perseverance the race that is set before

[25] John J. Pullen, The Twentieth Maine: A Volunteer Regiment in the Civil War (Philadelphia: J. B. Lippincott Co., 1957), p. 56.

us, looking to Jesus the pioneer and perfecter of our faith, who for the joy that was set before him endured the cross, despising the shame, and is seated at the right hand of the throne of God.

—Heb. 12:1-2

To the continuing fellowship of this glorious company the gospel calls us, and in this company we find power to cope victoriously with the contemporary crisis in character.

For Further Study

1. Books cited in the reference notes will supply abundant additional documentation of the crisis in character. Note particularly:

Cook, Fred J. *A Two Dollar Bet Means Murder.* New York: The Dial Press, Inc, 1961.

Gibney, Frank. *The Operators.* New York: Harper & Row, Publishers, 1959.

Starr, John. *The Purveyor: The Shocking Story of Today's Illicit Liquor Empire.* New York: Holt, Rhinehart & Winston, Inc., 1961.

The classic work on contemporary conformity is David Riesman's *The Lonely Crowd* (New Haven, Conn.: Yale University Press, 1950).

2. Consideration of this theme will surely issue in a sermon—or a series. Perhaps this is the place to note a basic principle of doctrinal preaching which should emerge here: Valid and effective preaching of doctrine begins with a need and brings the resources of a major Christian teaching to bear upon it. We have observed that a great conception of the church can speak powerfully to the crisis in character. This will be most likely to occur when the sermon starts, not with the doctrine of the church, but with the need. With the congregation, face the inner loneliness that makes us huddle into conformity to what others are doing and the tragic consequences that ensue. What will give us resources that liberate? Vast numbers of Christians find them in the church. What kind of church? From this can proceed the presentation of insights from scripture and doctrine, returning in every division of the sermon to the central thesis that this community of concern can liberate from loneliness and conformity by the strengthening bond of a larger fellowship in which we meet a divine Presence.

As you work on these preaching plans, do not forget to take the basic steps noted in the suggestions at the end of Chapter Five.

7
who speaks for freedom?

For the gospel interpreter some questions are inescapable. *Who Speaks for God?* asks Bishop Gerald Kennedy in the title of a significant book. That question is cardinal. No degree of devotion to "good causes" can replace the preacher's major commitment as spokesman of the Word. To make wise pronouncements, apart from that, is to vacate his central function. *Who Speaks for Man?* asks Norman Cousins, giving title to another important book. Nations have their spokesmen, as do parties, classes, ideologies, and races. But in the nuclear age, not these segments alone, but the future of humanity as a whole has come under threat. Yet mankind has no spokesman! Who, if not the interpreter of the good news that "God so loved the *world* . . . ," shall speak for man? Alongside these basic questions, another bids for place in the preacher's concern: Who speaks for freedom?

From its beginnings the gospel has been concerned with that. Hear Paul: "For freedom Christ has set us free; stand fast therefore, and do not submit again to a yoke of slavery" (Gal. 5:1). No code could bind the spirit of a man who had been set free by the love and forgiveness experienced in Christ. The choice was clear: either a man lives in the free response of a heart opened to God and his fellow men by the love awakened in him through God's gift in Christ, or he lives under bondage to some legalism. There is no middle ground. There can be no compromise. On this freedom he must stand.

The Reformation gave powerful re-emphasis to this theme. Luther found a key insight in Paul's words to the church at Corinth: "For he who was called in the Lord as a slave is a freedman of the Lord. Likewise he who was free when called is a slave of Christ" (I Cor. 7:22). No bondage to systems or institutions—neither to the social institution of slavery nor to the Church—can bind a man who belongs to God through Christ. Nor is any freedom real that is not based on inner discipline accepted under God as love's answer to Christ's forgiveness.

On this strategic ground at life's spiritual center the battle was first fought; but from the victory won there, other advances followed. Spiritual freedom had a corollary: Man cannot be held in any kind of bondage. Freedom to decide and to act is not a privilege any power can give or withhold. It is an inherent right. Political freedom, as implemented in American democracy, rests on two Christian insights. As a child of God, every man must be accorded the right of self-direction, so that government stands on authority jointly delegated by sovereign persons. And as a sinner, every man must be restrained from the presumptuous exercise of power at the expense of others, so that free government must be ensured by checks and balances among separated powers.

This creative nexus between religious faith and the demand for freedom from external bondage runs as deep in the Judeo-Christian heritage as the cry which God put on the lips of Moses: "Let my people go, that they may serve me" (Exod. 8:1, powerfully reiterated in ensuing chapters). Lifted in the name of God, linked to a religious purpose, the import of the demand was unmistakable—God's people must not be held in bondage. Small wonder that one of the most poignant of the spirituals wrung from the heart of the American Negro under slavery powerfully echoed that cry. Even Pharaoh saw the link, though he resisted the demand. "I do not know the Lord," he insisted, "and moreover I will not let Israel go" (Exod. 5:2). Both to the spokesman for a chartered liberty and to the preserver of a stubborn bondage, one truth was too obvious to deny—freedom and this faith in God would stand or fall together.

As James Russell Lowell, in another age when freedom was bitterly contested, saw that

> They are slaves who fear to speak,
> For the fallen and the weak,

so in our time three questions are part and parcel of one another: Who speaks for God? Who speaks for man? Who speaks for freedom?

II

The forces of tyranny and bondage have now mounted one of their most savage assaults. Bitterest in its violence in lands under Communism, it is not limited in geographic locale. Only in outward form does the attack increase or subside from year to year. In bewilderingly shifting guises it gives promise of continuing through the foreseeable future. In a resolution on civil liberties, the General Conference of The Methodist Church gave a concise and graphic description of the onslaught.

In this time of fear, areas of freedom of speech and thought are being narrowed all over the world. Everywhere there is increasing limitation of the expression of variant ideas and opinions, and even of factual information. Thought control uses the techniques of absolute censorship, surveillance by secret police, torture, imprisonment, and death. Other techniques are those of social rejection, calling of names, demands for "loyalty oaths," denial of employment, irresponsible accusations, and assertion of "guilt by association."

In any of these cases the results are false and inadequate information, degradation of the human mind, and shackling of the human spirit. In such an atmosphere suspicion becomes fear, fear becomes hatred, and hatred becomes war.[1]

---

[1] *Doctrines and Discipline of The Methodist Church, 1956* (Nashville: The Methodist Publishing House, 1957), p. 722.

In one of its most menacing manifestations this attack on freedom takes the form of brainwashing. An officer of the dictatorship portrayed in Karp's novel, *One*, expresses its strategy as he says to his victim, "I will pulverize your identity." Separating men from familiar surroundings and all communication with the world they have known, the brainwasher subjects them to an unrelenting stream of information, ideas, and stimuli totally at odds with their established outlooks and loyalties, until minds lose their moorings and are redirected along a course charted by the manipulators.

To a less extreme degree this experience is shared by many who have not fallen victim to dictatorship. On leave following his basic training in the Navy, a youthful recruit listened to a lecture on the technique of brainwashing. At its close he remarked that, in terms of his own recent experience, he could understand what had been said. He had endured nothing comparable, either in severity or in sinister purpose, to the ordeal the lecturer described; yet a similar principle had been at work. He had sent home his clothes, and been dressed in a fashion utterly strange to him. His hair had been cut in a way that made his reflection in the mirror almost unrecognizable. Plunged in an environment in many ways alien to all he had known, he had been played upon, day and night, by the conditioning of a new discipline and indoctrination. He retained his name, but in many ways his serial number was more important. In the cumulative weariness of grueling days at the accelerated pace, under these strange stimuli, he said, if someone had suddenly pointed a finger and asked, "Who are you, and where do you come from ?" he would have had to think hard to give his hesitant reply. Many a man shares similar recollections of military service.

Aldous Huxley draws a persuasive and spine-chilling picture of the possibilities of the extension of this technique to reshape whole societies, without their knowledge, into patterns they have not chosen. His prophetic fantasy of the world of scientifically conditioned people in a remote future century, drawn three decades ago in *Brave New World*, proved wrong only in the accelerated pace at which it came true. In the light of this prescience, his recent second thoughts in *Brave New World Revisited* command concerned attention.

Reflecting on the increasingly vast overpopulation of the earth, Huxley predicts that the pressure of such numbers upon available resources will lead to increasing regimentation to assure that all are supplied. The regimented peoples, he fears, will be drawn together into increasingly titanic power blocs ranged against one another in constant vigilance and mutual threat. Under this tension the United States would react to mounting insecurity by accelerated preparations for retaliation and defense. Personal liberties would be hard pressed. Permanent control of all aspects of the common life would be the expected by-product of warlike postures in a chronic state of crisis.

Under such conditions the Social Ethic, concerning which David Riesman, William H. Whyte, Jr., and others have written discerningly, would emerge into even greater prominence. Its emphasis on, and rationale for, conformity, togetherness, groupness, group dynamics, and group creativity would assign increasingly greater value to the social whole than to the parts it comprises. What happens when organization is held to outvalue persons, the world has seen under the regimes of Hitler and Stalin. In the new age, however, such concentration of power and regulation of life would come about more subtly and painlessly, through the methods of "social engineering."

Even under a democracy, Huxley notes, the control of opinion through the mass media is concentrated in fewer and fewer hands. The huge investments these media require enforce this concentration by eliminating smaller competitors. The struggle to capture a mass audience gives rise to a least common denominator of the unreal and the irrelevant, as distractions from unpleasant or taxing realities. Entertainment and the hypnotic suggestions of advertising edge out thought. Not even in Rome, with its bread and circuses, he says, was there anything like the nonstop distraction of our mass media. From what is now the fact in a democratic society, it is not a long step to the social engineers' manipulation of the mass mind under the pressures toward regimentation. Giving full play to the sophisticated techniques of emotionally charged words, subliminal stimulation, sleep-teaching, and numerous other psychological gadgets and "hidden persuaders," the engineers can carry on the tradition of public meetings and political conventions to arrive at predetermined and carefully managed outcomes. If we smile at such predictions now, Huxley warns, we may find them far less amusing a decade or two hence. Unless a great many people become aroused enough to be willing to take a good deal of trouble to reverse this trend, what now sounds like science fiction will become accomplished fact.

These predictions gain credibility not alone from their author's previous accuracy and the inherent forcefulness of his argument, but also from a trend in our history which prepares a climate for such developments. The manipulation of the mind by forces of blind emotionalism and irrationality has precedents in the Know Nothingism of an earlier period, and in the Ku Klux Klan outbursts, the McCarthyism, the John Birch Societies, and the irregularities of the House Committee on Un-American Activities in more recent times. The Un-American Activities Committee has persisted over a long period in a reversal of the practices on which the structure of civil liberties rests. It has heard witnesses without cross-examination or the hearing of available testimony on the other side; it has investigated without informing the accused of the charges or suspicions held against them; it has entered in the record, without notation of dates of alleged occurrences, evidence which would have been shorn of its damaging effect had the relevant dates been noted; and it has lumped this mass of unchecked accusations, suspicions, and inferences together in reports published under the official seal of the government, conveying to the uninformed or the unwary an impression of solemn judicial certainty. The denial of freedom could hardly be more explicit than the remark to a witness by the late J. Parnell Thomas, as chairman of the committee: "You have no rights except what this committee chooses to give you."

III

To the interpreter who takes seriously the charter of freedom at the gospel's heart, this trend, casting its long shadow over the years ahead, constitutes a mandate. In its resolution on civil liberties, the General Conference of The Methodist Church moved swiftly from the gospel assurance to the prophetic imperative. The resolution said:

We who are Christians profess that Christ came to demonstrate the character of God and reveal that God is love. Love is the power of God at work in human relations. Against such power no earthly barriers can stand, no earthly armies ultimately can prevail. This power can be ours. We need only dare to use it.[2]

But we do need that! Effective witness depends on sensitivity to the emergent issue, alertness to present responsibility. Subtle, but destroying, is the temptation to procrastinate until an issue is settled and one is saved the necessity of saying the uncomfortable word. How easy it is to appear to speak on an issue while falling just short of effective forthrightness, only the relentless conscience can discern. Maintaining unsurrendered the theory of a free pulpit while resorting frequently to expedient silence or to one or another of these ways of hedging, many a minister has been muzzled in all but the name. As one prophetic preacher declared, "The only way to have a free pulpit is to use it."

All men are the stronger in their freedoms for the courageous utterances of a few who have dared to speak at the place and moment when the word counted most. Every American has cause to be grateful to Bishop G. Bromley Oxnam for

[2] *Ibid.*, p. 722.

his masterful reply to the undemocratic procedures of Congressional committees, both in his own ordeal before the committee and in his effective reporting of it in his book *I Protest*. Christians throughout the world are indebted to Bishop Otto Dibelius for heroic resistance to official curtailments of religious liberty in East Germany. In a letter to Prime Minister Grotewohl, the bishop stood firmly for Christian principle against repressive onslaughts, as he wrote:

> The dialectic materialsm may say whatever it wishes when people are forced to take part in political demonstrations which they feel are not right. For the Christian this is an infringement upon his God-given human dignity. When in a constitution it is resoundingly declared that no person shall suffer any subsequent disadvantage if he speaks his opinion freely and openly, and then in practice exactly the opposite becomes a daily experience, this is for the Christian conscience a violation of trust and confidence.[3]

To obscure Christians who adhere to conviction at personal risk, all men who value freedom of the spirit stand obligated. Typical was the East German mother whose husband had disappeared in 1945, and who supported her children and her aged parents as a teacher. When it was required that she press her students to enroll for the atheistic indoctrination leading to the Communist Youth Dedication, she left her honored profession and took menial employment to support those dependent on her. Under such stringencies new meanings appear in old texts: "Whoever loses his life for my sake and the gospel's will save it." (Mark 8:35). "He who loves father or mother more than me is not worthy of me; and he who loves son or daughter more than me is not worthy of me." (Matt. 10:37.) In congregations enduring such trials Bishop Dibelius noted a quickened response to these challenges. With fresh understanding his people heard texts like these or the psalmist's words,

[3] As quoted in Solberg, *op. cit.*, p. 95.

Out of the depths I cry to thee, O Lord!
Lord, hear my voice!
                              —Ps. 130:1 [4]

Shall we who preach in America be exempt from the need to speak for freedom when it is infringed? That the test is less dramatic does not diminish its urgency. In many a community the violations of the rights of racial minorities in matters of housing, employment, and access to public facilities challenge the Christian conscience. The bold attacks of the John Birch Society and similar organs of neo-McCarthyism assail the free expression and open debate by which a strong democracy clears its mind. The springs of compassion are stopped by the bitterness of prejudice. Whether our inconspicuous protest can prevail against the forces of repression is not the crucial question. The East German witnesses could have no hope of changing the situation by their word or act, yet freedom everywhere is stronger because they were not silenced. One man who speaks stiffens the spirit in others. No man can tell when his lone witness will liberate and empower a mightier one. Nor are we ourselves free while counsels of expediency silence us in the face of the enemies of freedom.

They are slaves who fear to speak,
For the fallen and the weak,

IV

In a celebrated test case in 1894, the Board of Regents of the University of Wisconsin memorably stated the first article of a philosophy of freedom prerequisite to preaching in this field. In response to charges of heresy and sedition lodged against a professor of economics, the board held hearings in which it not only cleared the professor but affirmed a principle, concluding: "Whatever may be the limitations which trammel inquiry elsewhere, we believe that the great State University of Wisconsin should ever encourage that continual and fearless

[4] *Ibid.*, pp. 198 f, 153.

sifting and winnowing by which alone the truth can be found." [5]

This major premise stands on unassailable facts: that truths now widely held were once looked upon with universal doubt or open charges of heresy; that these truths won their way in the contest of discussion and debate in which they stood the tests failed by their rivals; that protection of what was regarded true yesterday by silencing what was considered false would have closed the door to discovery of truth now treasured. On the advancing frontier of knowledge, where our generation, like its predecessors, must edge forward step by step, this "fearless sifting and winnowing" is a perennial necessity. Seeing this, Thomas Jefferson declared: "If there be any among us who would wish to dissolve this Union or to change its republican form, let them stand undisturbed as monuments of the safety with which error of opinion may be tolerated where reason is left free to combat it." [6]

Beyond its confidence in the power of truth to establish itself in "a free market of ideas," an adequate philosophy of freedom holds that persons—whose sovereignty under God Christianity affirms and democracy makes the foundation of the state—can arrive at mature judgment befitting their sovereign responsibility only by exposure to all the winds of thought. They must hear both what may be true and what may be false, and make hard choices between them. In a tense episode in 1949, Dean Wilbur J. Bender of Harvard College held to this principle. Invited by a student organization, Gerhart Eisler, whose refusal to answer questions before the House Committee on un-American Activities had made him liable to fine and imprisonment, had spoken in Emerson Hall. When the urging of Fulton Lewis, Jr., evoked some three hundred letters of protest from his nationwide radio audience, Dean Bender issued a statement which said in part:

[5] Inscription on a plaque affixed to Bascom Hall on the campus of the University of Wisconsin, Madison, Wisconsin.

[6] Jefferson's First Inaugural Address.

The world is full of dangerous ideas, and we are both naïve and stupid if we believe that the way to prepare intelligent young men to face the world is to try to protect them from such ideas while they are in college. Four years spent in an insulated nursery will produce gullible innocents, not tough-minded realists who know what they believe because they have faced the enemies of their beliefs. We are not afraid of the enemies of democracy who are willing to express their ideas in the forum. . . . We have confidence in the strength of our free and dynamic American democracy. There is no danger from an open communist which is half as great as the danger from those who would destroy freedom in the name of freedom. . . . If Harvard students can be corrupted by an Eisler, Harvard College had better shut down as an educational institution.[7]

Confident of the power of truth to establish itself in an open contest of ideas, dedicated to the maturing of persons capable of responsible choice, a vital philosophy of freedom recognizes that freedom is most tested at the point of one's readiness to defend the right to be heard in the case of those with whom he most heartily disagrees. The association may be uncomfortable, but the necessity is clear. In the words of former President Harry S. Truman:

Almost always, the issues are raised over unpopular people or unpopular causes. In the cause of freedom, we have to battle for the rights of people with whom we do not agree; and whom, in many cases, we may not like. These people test the strength of the freedoms which protect all of us. If we do not defend their rights, we endanger our own.[8]

In our time a philosophy of freedom must cope at last with the suspicion that freedom itself is an illusion, and that,

[7] Reprinted from the Harvard Alumni *Bulletin* of March 12, 1949. Copyright 1949 by the Harvard Alumni Bulletin, Inc. Used by permission of W. J. Bender.

[8] From an address given by Mr. Truman at a dinner of the Four Freedoms Foundation in 1953, as quoted in Elmer Davis, *But We Were Born Free* (New York: The Bobbs-Merrill Company, Inc., 1954), p. 112.

despite all our struggles, it is beyond man's capability to be free. Concerning man Hamlet could exclaim, "How like a god!" But we who come in the wake of Pavlov are tempted to say, "How like a dog!" As Joseph Wood Krutch intimates, we have applied to the study of man methods first devised for the study of white rats or of machines; and it is not surprising that such methods discover in man only the traits he shares in common with these. To the question, "How much human behavior lies within the control of mechanical laws?" such studies return the answer, "Nearly all," and their enthusiasts then frequently overlook the *nearly*.[9]

Ironic inconsistencies appear in such thinking. It arrives at the conclusion that man cannot use the word *ought* in any meaningful sense indicative of obligation to choose responsibly between alternatives equally open and possible. There is no *ought* in this sense, it argues, since for men held in the grip of mechanical causation the outcome is predetermined, and choice itself is an illusion. But those who argue thus seem to be gripped by the conviction that they *ought* to state their case with the vigor its supposed truth deserves, and that sensible men hearing them *ought* to be convinced by the evidence and accept the conclusion.

For those who think thus, the word "truth" is drained of meaning. If men cannot choose responsibly; if every man must believe as mechanical factors condition him to believe, my truth is the product of the factors that condition me. By the same token my neighbor's opposite conclusion, being the product of the factors that condition him, has equal right to the status of truth for him. But a theory which gives equal standing to opposite conclusions, under the name of truth, arrives at the point where nothing is true in a recognizable meaning of that term. The suspicion that men cannot be free to make responsible choices thus ends where all skepticism ends, in

[9] Cf. Krutch, *op. cit.*, chap. I.

self-defeat and self-refutation; and a vital philosophy of freedom is left in possession of the field.

V

More imperative for preaching, however, is a theology of freedom. Philosophical arguments and propaganda devices are powerless to sustain the freedom of men at the center of whose lives is a spiritual vacancy. Such a psychic vacuum will not remain empty. Men who have no adequate sense of a Ground of Being in God cannot long endure without some fixed center of existence. Having denied God, they are presently won by some other absolute—dialectic materialism, perhaps, or a Nazi conception of the master race. Only a sense of belonging to a Purpose beyond one's own purpose, which invites loyal obedience, can ultimately underwrite freedom.[10] So central to a theology of freedom is Paul's declaration in Rom. 8:28-30 that Christian thinking cannot proceed in this area without coming to grips with it.

We know that in everything God works for good with those who love him, who are called according to his purpose. For those whom he foreknew he also predestined to be conformed to the image of his Son, in order that he might be the firstborn among many brethren. And those whom he predestined he also called; and those whom he called he also justified; and those whom he justified he also glorified.

To assert that God *foreknew* and *predestined* those whom he called is not to argue for a theory of determinism. The opening words sound the keynote: "We know that in everything God works for good with those who love him"—which takes for granted a relation which does not stifle the free action of men in response to God. Men can love God; and love is meaningless unless its alternative is also possible. For what significance can there be in a love which is compelled? Those

---

[10] For a fuller statement of this thesis cf. Thielicke, *op. cit.*, chap. XI.

who love God are pictured not in the iron grip of God's will, but working at tasks in which God works with them. No assurance is offered that only good things will happen to them. Existentialists like Sartre hold that life merely *happens to* men; this virile Christian outlook sees life rather as a co-operative venture chosen in loving obedience to God.

To Paul's statement, "Those whom he foreknew he also predestined to be conformed to the image of his Son," the contemporary mind replies with a question: Does not God's foreknowledge imply that our path was marked out beforehand with an inevitability which leaves no room for personal decision? William James met this inquiry with his analogy of the chess master. The master player foreknows his opponent's moves in the sense that he knows all possible moves in any given development of the game. He cannot tell with certainty which of the alternatives the novice will elect, but he foresees all that can happen on the board, and whatever develops he has the adequate answering move. Or, changing the figure, God does not pace the floor of heaven wringing his hands over affairs whose outcome remains in anxious doubt. His foreknowledge of his children is not unlike that of a mature and competent parent whose plan and provision for his children runs far ahead of the event.[11]

In the phrase, "predestined to be conformed to the image of his Son," Paul reflects a profound sense of participation in a corporate destiny. Israel had been predestined to fulfill a mission for which God had chosen them, and Paul had a deeply ingrained sense of participation in the life of his people. God had predestined the church to serve his purpose as the new Israel, and Paul was convinced of his participation in the body of Christ. In response to the transformation which comes through God's saving grace, Christian experience testifies, "It was all God"; but in the midst of life's emergent issues moral experience resolves, "I must act responsibly." Paul

[11] Cf. Krumm, *op. cit.*, pp. 162 f.

shared in both experiences and felt no conflict between them.[12]

When he wrote, "Those whom he predestined he also called," Paul brought the two poles of thought into one compact statement; for the call implies a responsible answer. Peter A. Bertocci suggests, in another context, that a well-brought-up child, for whom provisions have been made in a good school, music lessons, and other advantages, must finally choose the cultured life as his own. The passive "good boy" who does as a matter of course all that is expected of him, though it is no real affair of his own, is hopeless. "There is no fire in him!" [13] Similarly, Niebuhr points out that we are all elected to life, to humanity, and to our own selfhood quite without our choice; yet no one lives fully until he chooses life, the way of humanity, and a full acceptance of himself.[14] Cast in a mold of predestination, we are called to a response which can only be voluntary. To live fully is to choose life.

VI

Though themes urge themselves upon the preacher at every turn amidst such subject matter, let us examine only three suggestive approaches to the double analysis in which sermons come to life.

Paul's words in Rom. 8:15-16 propose the first of these, an aggravated contemporary quandry. "For you did not receive the spirit of slavery to fall back into fear," he writes, "but you have received the spirit of sonship. When we cry, 'Abba! Father!' it is the Spirit himself bearing witness with our spirit that we are children of God." This returns us to the crucial question of our identity, which confronted us in Chapter I and has emerged repeatedly along the way we have come. Machines intimidate us. Hypnotic awe of electronic com-

---

[12] The treatment of this passage in *The Interpreter's Bible*, it will be noted, supports this point of view.

[13] *Free Will, Responsibility, and Grace* (Nashville: Abingdon Press, 1957), p. 76.

[14] *Christ and Culture* (New York: Harper & Row, Publishers, 1951), pp. 249 f.

puters holds us in its spell. Are we children of God? The shadow of the machine obscures our perception of ourselves in his image; and if it prevails, our responsible use of freedom is doomed.

Tom Watson, Jr., who as president of IBM may be presumed to know something about computers, opens a door worth entering. "Man," he declares, "has made some machines that can answer questions provided the facts are previously stored in them, but he will never be able to make a machine that will ask questions. . . . The ability to ask the right questons is more than half the battle of finding the right answer." [15] Such questions, perhaps, as, "What is man that thou art mindful of him, and the son of man that thou dost care for him?" (Ps. 8:4.) Or, "How much more is a man worth than a sheep?" (Matt. 12:12 Moffatt.) Or, "Do you not know that you are God's temple and that God's Spirit dwells in you?" (I Cor. 3:16.)

Keep these questions clear, and no image of the machine can rob you of the freedom that is your birthright as a child of God.

Moses' demand, "Let my people go" (Exod. 5:1) issued in the name of God, opens a second avenue of consideration. It boldly assumes a right to command which rests with a divine Order above all human orders. The trial of Adolph Eichmann brought into focus the pressing immediacy of this issue. Eichmann did not deny that he had given orders which led to the death of great numbers of Jews; yet he pled innocence on the ground that he did only what he, in turn, had been commanded. This modern plea, that guilt or innocence can be transferred to another from whom an order is received, rests back at last upon the state, and the belief that above the state there is no order.[16] In his demand, "Let my people go!" Moses

---

[15] As quoted in *Christian World Facts*, 1958-59, p. 17.

[16] It is somewhat shocking to find the dilemma posed by the Eichmann trial transferred to an American Civil War setting in the Broadway play, *The Andersonville Trial*.

refused to accept this claim. Unless Moses was right, the world is condemned to permanent disorder born of the anarchy which prevails when a collection of unrelated orders are in conflict. Only those who choose the way of obedience to the one supreme Order can live in the freedom of a world at peace.

Helmut Thielicke suggests that dictatorship does not produce human robots; human robots produce dictatorship. Where the mere functionary has replaced the person grounded in his identity as child of God, dictatorship is almost sure to follow. When standards sag because life is rooted in no divine Order, the unified life of society ravels out into innumerable fraying strands of individual existence, each going his own way. Into the chaos of such disintegrated life the dictator comes to restore a semblance of order—until he, too, runs afoul of the world chaos which is inevitable when he recognizes no Order above his own.[17] Against the apocalyptic disasters to which all this leads, we have a bulwark: "Thus says the Lord, 'Let my people go, that they may serve me' " (Exod. 8:1).

There is, finally, a word of judgment without which freedom always lives a hunted life. Pertinent is the oracle of Isaiah:

> The Lord has taken his place to contend,
>   he stands to judge his people.
> The Lord enters into judgment
>   with the elders and princes of his people:
> "It is you who have devoured the vineyard,
>   the spoil of the poor is in your houses.
> What do you mean by crushing my people,
>   by grinding the face of the poor?"
>   says the Lord of hosts.
>   —Isa. 3:13-15

Here the judgment of God and the rights of the poor are so linked that their freedom may not be violated with impunity.

[17] Thielicke, op. cit., p. 80.

Today the issue is insistent. To the secularist nurtured in the indifferent atmosphere of the Genial Society, as to the Christian with a superficial impression of the theology of grace, judgment seems far removed. And apart from judgment there is no enduring freedom. For if men are judged by no transcendent standard, authority is free to assert itself with no limit but its whim or the boundaries set by conflict with other authorities. Then power becomes its own justification. If it is true, however, that "The Lord has taken his place to contend, he stands to judge his people," there is great good news for the oppressed.

Judgment is the other side of grace. A God without judgment for Hitler would be a God without love for six million murdered Jews. Nothing could so tell the sad news that family love is dead, as does an uncaring indifference whether wife or husband or children do well or ill. To love is to care intensely when a loved one does wrong. To shrug off evil with a nonchalant, "It doesn't matter," is to admit plainly that one does not love. For judgment is love's other face. In God this is supremely true; the judgment that puts ultimate limits on evil is the other side of grace that leads to the fullest, freest life.

For Further Study

1. For an excellent source book of basic documents to sharpen thinking and provide luminous illustration on this subject, *Primer of Intellectual Freedom*, edited by Howard Mumford Jones (Cambridge, Mass.: Harvard University Press, 1949) is unsurpassed. *The Measure of Man*, by Joseph Wood Krutch (New York: The Bobbs-Merrill Company, 1954) struggles for a non-deterministic view of man from the point of view of a noble humanism. Somewhat the same philosophical problem is considered on theistic grounds in *Free Will, Responsibility, and Grace*, by Peter A. Bertocci (Nashville: Abingdon Press, 1957). The books by Aldous Huxley and Bishop G. Bromley Oxnam referred to in the text of this chapter will repay thoughtful reading.

2. As you prepare to preach on an aspect of this theme most pertinent to a need or question you sense among your people, remember this recent challenge of an "outsider" to the Christian spokesman:

"If you have anything distinctively Christian to say to this dangerous predicament we are in, for God's sake say it. If you have nothing to say that could not be heard on a street corner or at a luncheon club, for God's sake keep still." The distinctively Christian word on freedom has a courageous forthrightness, but it has a dimension of depth that takes it far beyond exhortation. Be sure you capture that distinctively Christian word—which means your message must be carefully grounded in Scripture approached (1) by diligent exegesis, and (2) by alert double analysis. It also means that your work with the Scripture must be paralleled by the statement of the sermon's central idea, or proposition, in a single sentence which relates freedom to the good news of God. When you have your outline planned, you should re-examine it, asking: Does every division of this outline have an obvious relation to the central proposition? How can I make the connection even more clear?

8
creative christians confront crisis

A snatch of conversation opening the thirteenth chapter of the Gospel according to Mark sounds strangely at home in our crisis-threatened time. Pointing to the great stones of the temple, one of the disciples spoke with pride in what his people had been able to accomplish: "Look, Teacher, what wonderful stones and what wonderful buildings!" "Do you see these great buildings?" Jesus replied. "There will not be left here one stone upon another, that will not be thrown down." (Mark 13:1-2.) Thrusting our skyscrapers against the sky and projecting voyages to the moon, we share the disciples' pride in our "great stones." And the answer, "not one stone upon another," sends a shudder through us by its twentieth-century realism. A distinguished journalist sounds his warning in a book titled *Two Minutes Till Midnight*; a famed missionary publishes a message *Wake Up or Blow Up!*; and the dean of world statesmen speaks of an age living under a "balance of terror." To minds formed in such a time only a gospel prepared to cope with crisis can carry conviction.

The conversation we have quoted introduces the famous "little apocalpse." To use this term is to be reminded that what follows represents a strand of the message having distinguishing characteristics of its own. We now know enough about the widespread literary fashion of apocalyptic writing in the first century to make due allowance for its typical patterns. Its florid figures of speech spoke to the mood of a desperate moment in history, using literary allusions deliberately designed to convey to the mind steeped in Hebrew culture, meanings which would be missed by the pagan overlords. It adopted honored pseudonyms, issuing its message in the names of prophetic leaders, as the early church may have put on the lips of Jesus the deep convictions expressed in this chapter. It held a deterministic view of history, at variance from that of the prophets: these events will inevitably transpire under the mighty hand of God, said the apocalyptists; these events will transpire unless the people repent, said the prophets. To make allowance for these traits is not only to recognize the departure of apocalyptic from the mind of the prophets, or its strangeness to the more prosaic mood of our time; it is also to see how alien it was to the later New Testament faith represented by the Fourth Gospel. For in John our Lord's return is described not in this lurid cosmic imagery, but as the coming of "the Spirit of truth, whom the world cannot receive, because it neither sees him nor knows him" (John 14:17).

When all allowance has been made, however, this "little apocalypse" carries a valid reflection of how fully Jesus shared the viewpoint and manner of speaking deeply embedded in the communication of his time. "God had made the world and could bring its history to an end when he chose; and the Kingdom of God would surely come." [1] Jesus seems to have predicted the fall of the temple; and if he did not speak of future events in the exact terms introduced by the literary style of this chapter, he undoubtedly did issue its call to be ready at all times for the day of God's judgment. To our apocalyptic time, this chapter speaks powerfully of God's unfailing control and of our call to live creatively in crisis.

We need such assurance. Informed reporters tell us that a single B-52 flying an airborne alert carries blast power equal to more than twelve times the total of the explosives dropped in World War II, including the two atomic bursts

---

[1] Sherman E. Johnson, *Commentary on the Gospel According to St. Mark* (New York: Harper & Row, Publishers, 1960), p. 219. The viewpoint here expressed on the validity of the apocalyptic in Mark is substantiated in detail by Johnson's sharp analysis in this contribution to the Harper's New Testament Commentaries,

at Hiroshima and Nagasaki.[2] To anyone who has walked through the miles of devastation of a major city, or witnessed such a tragic symbol as the mass grave of 60,000 victims of a single bombing raid on Hamburg, that is a statement full of unspeakable horror. Recognized authorities estimate that the first sixty days of all-out nuclear war between the United States and Russia in the mid-1960's would kill 140,000,000 Americans and number the Russian casualties in the range of 85 to 90 per cent of their population.[3] Death would spread its mantle over many other countries in the process. Those who were spared would face a struggle beyond the limits of imagination—frightful disorders; the breakdown of sanitation, communication, and vital public services; widespread crop failures; malnutrition, homelessness, vast epidemics.

Could a faith bereft of its apocalyptic outlook speak to such a time? How aptly descriptive of the threats that hang over us is the message this chapter remembers!

Let him who is on the housetop not go down, nor enter his house, to take anything away; and let him who is in the field not turn back to take his mantle. And alas for those who are with child and for those who give suck in those days! Pray that it may not happen in winter. For in those days there will be such tribulation as has not been from the beginning of the creation which God created until now, and never will be.

—Mark 13:15-19

To such a time Jesus spoke of God unfailingly in control, his people called to use crisis creatively. That is good news for our numbed minds.

For all its apocalyptic frightfulness, war is only one aspect of the crisis through which every trembling mortal must make his way. Crisis is continuous. The temple did not fall by nuclear attack, but it fell. Those who heard the message then, those who have heard it through intervening centuries, did not

[2] Arthur T. Hadley, *The Nation's Safety and Arms Control* (New York: The Viking Press, Inc., 1961), p. 4.
[3] *Ibid.*, p. 33 ff.

die by radiation, but they died. However it comes, death is the universal leveler. Disabling sickness comes crashing into many a home, devastatingly changing everything. Reverses lay waste our best laid plans. The realism of the marriage service —"for better, for worse, for richer, for poorer, in sickness and in health . . . till death us do part"—is essential to any sane handling of life. For those who are ready only for sunny days are not ready to live. In the double analysis necessary to valid preaching, the gospel speaks to our crises. Events have not outrun God's competence and control, it says; in the power of that faith we can meet crisis creatively.

II

Only as it builds on God as unshakable certainty in the midst of our shattered securities, can the message to this time have anything adequate to say. "And when they bring you to trial and deliver you up," runs the Gospel's graphic assurance, "do not be anxious beforehand what you are to say; but say whatever is given you in that hour, for it is not you who speak, but the Holy Spirit." (Mark 13:11.) By now, one trusts, we have outlived the misuse of these words as validation of a bargain-basement theory of preaching to justify skimped preparation. One distinguished theologian voiced what most thoughtful preachers have discovered—that the Holy Spirit never had said anything to him in the pulpit not previously said in his study, save on one occasion when in the concluding moments of a weak sermon there came the distinct message, "You have been lazy!" The exploding of a silly theory about this passage, however, ought not to deafen us to its true and strengthening word.

Spoken first to those who were to face persecution, as an assurance that by the power of God the gospel could stand in the face of all enemies, it comes with a new aptness to such a time as ours. The tragic experience of concentration camps has made it clear that those who best survive hardships are not the calloused who possess great physical strength, who are often outlived by the physically weak who have great inner resources. Olin Stockwell, surviving years in a Chinese Communist prison by the power of a faith that inspired a vital book of devotions minutely written on the margins of his New Testament, and the composition of hymns memorized as created for want of paper to which to commit them, was only one of a numerous heroic company who have endured the impossible through this power.

In such strange and terrible circumstances God remains our home, as the psalmist proclaimed:

> Lord, thou hast been our dwelling place
> in all generations.
> —Ps. 90:1

A widely shared experience with the stars is but a shadow of this unshaken sense of home. A boy explored his way about the sky on a path blazed by constellations and brighter stars he had learned to identify; and as a man he looked up from the streets of strange cities and the churning waters of wilderness rivers, in his homeland and in far countries, in times placid and turbulent, and was less bewildered by strangeness because his old friends were there. In a way deeper and truer, men have found an unfailing strength and a home in far places as they have committed their ways anew to God in prayer.

A German pastor recounts such an experience as, following imprisonment in Russia, he made his way home, mostly on foot, at the war's end, desperately homesick and uncertain as to whether his wife and children had survived. Passing a peasant home where a boy and girl were playing, and wanting some bit of conversation with them because of their likeness to his own children, he asked the question most normal in those uprooted times: "Are you evacuated?" "No," replied the lad, with a child's ambiguous understanding, "we're Evangelicals." Then the children turned and ran into their father's house. "And," the pastor added, "with their words, 'We're Evangelicals,' ringing in my ears, I went on my way less lonely in the realization that the whole world is my Father's house.

Building on that certainty, we can live and help others live in crisis, confident that when evil and death have done their worst, Spirit and life will possess the field. In the vivid words of the Gospel, "Brother will deliver up brother to death, and the father his child, and children will rise against parents and have them put to death; and you will be hated by all for my name's sake. But he who endures to the end will be saved" (Mark 13:12-13). Neither Jesus nor his first followers could ever speak with light bravado of death; they lived too intimately with it, and its grizzly challenge too constantly confronted them. Yet at every turn his conscious grip on victory over it rang out. "Today," he told a companion in crucifixion, "you will be with me in Paradise" (Luke 23:43). To Martha's wistful hope of a future resurrection he replied with an assured present tense: "I am the resurrection and the life" (John 11:25). In his farewell to the disciples, he said: "In my Father's house are many rooms. . . . And when I go and prepare a place for you, I will come again and will take you to myself, that where I am you may be also" (John 14:2-3).

To those in our crisis-gripped generation who are inclined to doubt his assurance, no proof is offered. Argument is insufficient to dissuade unwilling minds from the suspicion that he may have been mistaken. But beyond that misgiving another word must be heard. Leslie Weatherhead put it with power. Jesus may have been mistaken about this vital matter on which he spoke often and vigorously—as Shakespeare may have been mistaken as to what constitutes a sonnet, or Chopin and Beethoven on what makes good music, or Turner about the elements of a picture. In this realm he is the Expert. In these matters his insight so far outruns all others that, though we admit the theoretical possibility that he may have been wrong, to do so involves presumption bordering on absurdity. We may not have proof, but faith stands on solid ground when it nails to the mast the conviction that God has the final word over death and evil, not only in this world and within the limits of time, but in all worlds and eternally. That note must vibrate through any preaching that sustains men in the crisis of the mid-twentieth century.

III

Confident of God's undeviating control and unfailing love, the Gospel calls to a creative use of crisis. Nothing in the cosmic sweep of the Gospel apocalypse is more characteristic of the mind of Jesus than its concluding emphasis, "Take heed, watch; for you do not know when the time will come" (Mark 13:33). Set in the context of the parable of the fig tree, on reading the signs of the times, and the parable of the sudden return of the householder, with its call to constant readiness, this emphasis is underscored a second time: "And what I say to you I say to all: Watch" (Mark 13:37). Read the times, it seems to say, but do not dissipate your energies in anxious speculation. Be ready at all times. Crises break old patterns. After bereavement, or penitence, or tempation, or any other crisis, no man remains the same. New possibilities open. God calls to creative reconstruction.

Strong forces have converged on the pulpit to silence this note in a generation which most needs to hear it. Rediscovery of man's essential sinfulness has deepened the doubt that anything we can do about the human situation can survive the destructive taint that runs through human motives. A suspicion of illusory and presumptuous perfectionism has attached itself to our efforts to correct the evils that corrupt our systems. The forces which threaten to erupt are so gigantic, the complexities of the problems so bewildering, that a sense of helplessness overwhelms us, which on theological grounds is often regarded not as a counsel of doubt but as itself an article of faith. The editor of the *Saturday Review* has sounded a warning to a pulpit caught in the vortex of such forces. Climaxing his list of the enemies who must be overcome if we are to survive the crisis of this time, he names the man in the pulpit who withdraws into a message aimed only to provide individual comfort and refinement. Such a man, he declares,

talks about the sacredness of life but he never relates that concept to the real and specific threats that exist today to such sacredness. He identifies himself as a man of God but feels no urge to speak out against a situation in which the nature of man is likely to be altered and cheapened, the genetic integrity of man punctured, and distant generations condemned to a lower species. He is a dispenser of balm rather than the awakener of conscience. He is preoccupied with the need to provide personal peace of mind rather than to create a blazing sense of restlessness to set things right. He is an enemy because the crisis today is as much a spiritual crisis as it is a political one.[4]

Indeed the spiritual and the political now meet and interpenetrate. Erich Fromm points out how failure to solve the problem of war and nuclear arms exacts a spiritual toll. It makes barbarians of a whole population, he says, "though barbarians equipped with the most complicated machines." For this is the psychological outcome of living over an extended period "under the constant threat of destruction." Such prolonged condition produces "fright, hostility, callousness, a hardening of the heart, and a resulting indifference to all the values we cherish."[5] Our belief in spiritual forces—freedom, personal dignity, a God who is more than an empty idol—is undermined. We lose any depth of conviction about what we are *for*, and live by our hatred of what we are *against*. "If we continue to live in fear of extinction and to plan mass destruction of others, the last chance for a revival of our humanist-spiritual tradition will be lost."[6]

[4] Norman Cousins, *In Place of Folly* (New York: Harper & Row, Publishers, 1961), p. 208. Used by permission.

[5] Donald G. Brennan (ed.), *Arms Control, Disarmament, and National Security* (New York: George Braziller, Inc., 1961). Used by permission of *Daedalus* and the American Academy of Arts and Sciences. P. 190. Erich Fromm's article quoted here is only one of the numerous authoritative chapters in this brilliant symposium.

[6] *Ibid.*, p. 191.

Thus forthrightly do the leaders in the natural and behavioral sciences address the burning issue of survival for all that is most distinctly human. They know, as Lillian Smith said in another context, that silence is "our gift to the demagogue." Shall the Christian pulpit not bring the full power of religious conviction to bear on a matter so crucial? If not, the courageous humanists will be like the son in Jesus' parable, who said, "I will not," but still obeyed his father's intent; while we who speak in God's name resemble the son who answered, "I go, sir," but did not act. And our proper theological proclamation will lose its power to convince, because our witness has lost the persuasiveness of vital relevance.

IV

Yet it is precisely on central theological grounds that the Christian messenger is called to speak to the issues of war and the potential mass destruction inherent in the weapons of terror now being amassed by the nations. He takes his stand on faith in "God the Father almighty, maker of heaven and earth." Because creation is God's handiwork, men have no right to corrupt its forces and blight the resources of the good earth. God, who stored vast nuclear energies in radioactive materials, will not allow his creatures with impunity to twist these powers, from the creative purposes which destined them to be healers of disease and multipliers of the resources for abundant living, to the demonic intent of raining death upon the helpless and the innocent.

In the name of the Creator, we must call a halt to a reversal of his benign process, so horrible that by our pollution of the human genes we are now preparing the way for the birth of malformed children in generations yet to come. In reverence for the God who holds all ages in his keeping, we must make an end of the arrogance which—for purposes that, like all things human, are but for a day—flings into the atmosphere radioactive dust which will continue to spread disease and death for eight thousand years to come.[7] In the name of the God who is the giver and sustainer of life, we must desist from preparations for a war in which, as major scientists now foresee, "none of us would have enough living to bury our dead." [8]

The Christian messenger—who speaks in the name of the Lord of history—deals in matters that are not marginal to his call, when he addresses himself to history's unfolding pattern in this crucial age. To suppose that God's Lordship in human affairs awaits a remote future fulfillment of the prophecy that the kingdoms of this earth shall become the kingdoms of our Lord and of his Christ, is to miss the meaning of his sovereignty. For history, as Herbert Butterfield has said, is not like a train, which fulfills its purpose only in arriving at its destination. It is, rather, like a Beethoven symphony, the beauty of which does not wait until the final bar to reveal itself, but unfolds in each moving moment of music.[9] To serve the God of history is not to wait passively for the working out of his purpose in some far-off day of his visitation, but to respond to him with obedient action in each decisive present.

Such response calls for full participation in the risks of action aimed to promote the emergence of a more ordered world from the anarchy of this chaotic age. History's movement is toward the extension of order under law. Though the gospel forbids equating any human order or institution with the kingdom of God; though indeed all human institutions must be held under judgment by his kingdom; it is the part of responsible service in his name to lend support to all efforts to make the United Nations a fully effective instrument of world order.

This need not wait for sweeping Charter revision. It can evolve through day-to-day decisions. The movement to give

[7] Cousins, op. cit., p. 24.
[8] Brennan, op. cit., p. 452.
[9] *Christianity and History* (New York: Charles Scribner's Sons, 1950), p. 67.

greater responsibilities to the General Assembly and the Secretariat, thus escaping the paralysis that inheres in the veto, is a step in this direction. So, too, can be the growth of world law through judicial decisions as the International Court of Justice, possibly supplemented by regional courts provided for in the statute, comes into increasing use by the great powers.[10] While we move through these developments, there must be steady insistence on the reduction of armaments which have become not so much means for the arbitrament of disputes as threats to "the very existence of civilization and humanity." [11] For purposes of enforcement of its collective decisions, the world community—which has already protected order in repeated emergencies by use of a United Nations Emergency Force—can strengthen order by establishing a permanent international military force.

If these proposals seem visionary and utopian, it must be remembered that they merely extend the normal growth of processes already begun by more than one hundred nations acting in concert; and that the alternatives now are international anarchy represented in a continued armaments race leading to almost inevitable catastrophe, on the one hand; and the development of the "habit of law" into an ordered world community, on the other. To act responsibly in such developments, under motivations provided by Christian faith, is to render obedience to the God of history.

Not only on faith in "God the Father almighty" does the Christian messenger take his stand, but on the commitment to "Jesus Christ, his only Son, our Lord." This is the heart of the gospel. A minister invited to preach in a college chapel and to interpret what he considered the vital core of the Christian faith, took as a text the words in which Paul explained to King Agrippa his reason for living: "And I said, 'Who are you, Lord?' And the Lord said, 'I am Jesus whom you are persecuting'" (Acts 26:15), with its sequel: "I was not disobe-

---

[10] Brennan, op. cit., pp. 427 f.
[11] Ibid., p. 411.

dient to the heavenly vision" (Acts 26:19). Here is the turning point in the life of history's most creative Christian personality, seen not in a code of acts to perform, nor in a creedal statement of articles to believe, but in a new outlook, a new loyalty, a new relationship centered in Jesus Christ. Taking a cue from Bishop Anders Nygren, the preacher declared that in the person of Christ we find our most dependable *understanding* of the nature of the eternal, in comparison with him we come under the *judgment* of the eternal, through him we find both *reconciliation* with the eternal, and *power* to live by the claims of the eternal.[12]

This is what Bishop Nygren calls it, the *Essence of Christianity;* but when one has said this, he has not said all that is necessary in preaching the Christian message—as the minister was reminded when, in the question period that followed the chapel service, a young man said: "Granting that Christianity is neither a code nor a creed, but a personal relation, what is the relevance of that to the bitter circumstances of the present world in which we are called to act?" Faced with a question so proper and pertinent, what can one do but examine the motives to which Jesus makes appeal, and inquire into their implications concerning these crisis years?

Jesus told the parable of the good Samaritan in answer to a question concerning the great commandment. By so doing he elevated the need of another man—any other man, so long as he is in need—to a place of central concern. Is that not crucially relevant to our expenditure, in the face of the abject poverty which holds two thirds of humanity in its grip, of $25,000,000,000 a year for weapons of destruction and more than $8,000,000,000 annually in research designed to discover ways to multiply their deadliness? [13] Jesus told the parable of the judgment to say that life's crucial issue hinges on what

[12] This is a greatly simplified condensation of the theme Nygren develops in *Essence of Christianity*, trans. Philip S. Watson (Philadelphia: Muhlenberg Press, 1961).

[13] Brennan, *op. cit.*, p. 453.

we do to "the least of these" his brethren. Has that no imperative relevance to the attempt to stabilize world order by a kind of "deterrence" which a leading strategic expert estimates might be triggered into warfare in which "both the United States and NATO would reluctantly envisage the possibility of one or two hundred million fatalities (i.e., about five times more than those in World War II) from the immediate effects, even if one does not include long-term effects due to radiation"? [14] To preach Christ compellingly to the contemporary mind is to bring the motives of Jesus to bear realistically upon such issues.

Preaching in this crisis, the Christian messenger depends on the guidance of the Holy Spirit. By the action of the Spirit, the Church has been called into being as a people of God actively engaged in and with the world God seeks to save. As such a people, we are called to witness not only by our words but by our acts, which must include responsible participation in the decisions which spell weal or woe for millions of God's children. As God's people, we live in constant awareness of mystery, which must warn us against the arrogance of equating our ideas with God's plan. As God's people, we live under the demand of obedience, which forbids equally that we enforce our will as if it were God's, or withhold our action when God speaks to our conscience.

By the power of the Spirit we face the frightening tasks involved in living creatively in crisis. In the face of such demands there is a deadly temptation to suppose that if we cannot do the whole task of building the better world for which we pray, there is no good in attempting anything—as when Lloyd George declared that the most dangerous feat in the world is the attempt to get across a chasm in *two jumps*. Arthur Larson was not using theological language, but he was talking about the courage the Spirit inspires, when he said in reply to that dictum: "If the longest distance you can leap is fifteen feet, and if the chasm is a hundred feet across, one leap can be rather dangerous too, and it might be better if you walked down and climbed up a step at a time." [15] That is the prospect held before us by the contemporary crisis, and for that gruelling task—which must be renewed undramatically day after day—the power of the Spirit is our reliance.

Yet the demand for daily diligence in small faithfulnesses must never induce cowardice in the face of necessity for reforms that cut to the heart of the great issues of arms reduction and world order. As John Stuart Mill once said, "Against a great evil, a small remedy does not produce a small result; it produces no result at all." [16] By the power of the Spirit the people of God can dare to attempt the great remedies demanded by the great evils of this age.

V

Under our Lord's injunctions to "watch," the Christian who takes seriously the call to live creatively in crisis feels the pull of the rights of people of all races. Concern with a question so near the center of the Christian doctrine of man must run deeper than its bearing on the international dangers that confront us. Yet these dangers focus attention on the race issue as one frought with judgment. The new status of the non-white majority of the world's peoples raises sharp questions concerning our race practices and their probable outcome in world relations. In an address to newsmen in the nation's capital, Edward R. Murrow asked:

Where do we house African diplomats in our capital? These are representatives of Negro nations led by Negro leaders. It is bad enough that they read headlines of bus burnings and beatings. It is even worse that they find it near impossible to live in the capital of our nation. Landlords will not rent to them; schools refuse their children; stores will not let them try on clothes; beaches bar their families.

[15] *Ibid.*, p. 436.
[16] *Ibid.*, p. 456.

This is not something the Communists do to us. We do it ourselves in our own capital. Is it possible that we concern ourselves too much with outer space and far places, and too little with inner space and near places? [17]

That last phrase pinpoints this as a gospel concern. "Inner space" is the preacher's native domain, dealing as it does with attitudes which degrade both those against whom contemptuous prejudices are held, and those who hold them. "Near places"—does not the phrase point the minister to the discriminatory practices within his own parish, about which he cannot be silent without dereliction of duty? Concerning such attitudes and practices the preacher needs to keep current in his diagnosis of the need to which he preaches. What race groups, and in what numbers, are present in the community? Are these groups present in the church in like ratio? What is their local access to housing, to employment commensurate with their abilities, to education, to medical and other services? If nonwhite racial groups are absent from the community, what local practices or "unwritten laws" account for that fact? What do the people of the congregation know about race? How much are their attitudes based on misinformation? These matters have been committed to the minister as a part of his spiritual trust, and he can interpret the gospel effectively only if he speaks out of accurate knowledge of this all-important inner space and these near places.

In his double analysis the preacher cannot neglect sociological concerns, but it must constantly be clear that the powerful thrust of his message is drawn from the central realities of the gospel. There is a core of biblical truth which runs through our message on race and human rights. The Bible is clear in its teaching that all men are created in God's image (Gen. 1:27); that God is the one Father to whom all men are invited to pray (Matt. 6:9); that God created all men in basic unity (Acts

---

[17] As quoted in the *Saturday Review*, XLIV, No. 23 (1961), p. 28. Used by permission of Mr. Murrow and *Saturday Review*.

17:26); that God's loving invitation is extended to all men (John 3:16); that all who confess Christ are bound in brotherhood (Philem. 16); that through Christ all divisions among men are transcended (Gal. 3:28; Col. 3:11); that all men are sinners, but God's grace overcomes sin for all men—including the sins of discrimination and division (II Cor. 5:17-19); that a general reconciliation is to be expected among men who are reconciled to God (II Cor. 5:20); and that Pentecost opened the doors of the church to all men so completely that since that event no man could open them wider and no man can close them save by parting company with the church's Lord (Acts 2:7-11; 10:9-16).

Far from a collection of proof texts, this amounts to a weighty cumulative consensus of the Scriptures on the way in which, in matters central to Christian experience and belief, the gospel holds all men in a unity so vital that race pales into insignificance. The Second Assembly of the World Council of Churches summed up the conviction of Christendom's most representative ecumenical body that

any form of segregation based on race, colour or ethnic origin is contrary to the gospel, and is incompatible with the Christian doctrine of man and with the nature of the Church of Christ. The Assembly urges the churches within its membership to renounce all forms of segregation or discrimination and to work for their abolition within their own life and within society.[18]

When the gospel calls Christian men and women to watchful vigilance in the presence of massive evils, it requires more than generalized good will. Jesus enjoined his disciples to be as wise as serpents as well as harmless as doves. Some years ago the Moral Rearmament movement published its message through a series of portrayals of the frightful evils of our time—bombed cities, race disorders, labor troubles—followed by an appealing picture of a little child, with the caption,

[18] W. A. Visser 't Hooft (ed.), *The Evanston Report* (New York: Harper and Brothers, 1954), p. 158.

"She knows the answer." Such a message is oversimplified. Jesus commended the humility and teachable openness of children, but not their knowledge or their answers to complex and vital questions. The disciple is called to grow "to mature manhood, to the measure of the stature of the fulness of Christ" (Eph. 4:13). The interpreter of the message must face the complexities of a catastrophic time with moral earnestness and probing realism concerning concrete situations in which those who hear it are involved.

VI

Travelers in central Europe amid the desolation that followed World War II were impressed by islands of hope in the drab sea of despair. There were church-sponsored programs of sharing, vigorous hospital services carrying on their work against heavy odds, bright refugee villages in marked contrast with the gray hopelessness of the official refugee camps. In some of these agencies one encountered the familiar wall motto of German piety, which reads in translation, "We do not know what is coming, but we know who is coming—Christ." Where the human spirit most promptly and victoriously recovered its capacity to meet the ordeal of a shattered world, it was sustained and strengthened by the hope that motto declared.

It is the hope enshrined in the apocalyptic strand of the gospel, a hope which can be interpreted in terms of crude, naïve expectations, to be sure, but a hope which holds in its heart a mighty truth: the God whose lordship is seen in history stands also at the end of history. He is the Savior who sustains our efforts, but he is also the Judge who assesses outcomes. He is the God of all finalities, to whom faithful men can pray: "Abide with us in the end of the day, in the end of our life, in the end of the world." [19] His creative act underlies the human enterprise; his sovereign rule decrees that evil shall

[19] John W. Doberstein, *Minister's Prayer Book* (Philadelphia: Muhlenberg Press, 1959), p. 52, quoted from *Das Gebet der Tageszeiten*.

not finally have its way; his saving judgment stands at the end of all things as the final vindication of the meaningfulness of the struggle. At the end, as at the beginning, goodness and power are one; "What is highest in spirit is also deepest in nature."

Preaching must hold this mighty hope before our apocalyptic age. Psychiatrists have analyzed the death wish of *Man Against Himself,* and penetrating students of human affairs have suggested that two world wars and the build-up toward a third may well be the expression of a deep-lying suicidal drive gripping whole societies. Theologians have pointed out that it is far more than coincidence that all this moves on toward its climax in an age when, for great masses of men, life's center has been bereft of any meaning rooted in vital faith. To preach savingly in such a time we must find the way to make that faith convincingly real once more. Regaining God, men can regain their own sense of significant selfhood; and recovering that, they have a secure footing in their struggle with the vast and complex forces they must meet. The call to the creative use of crisis is a call to relentless and realistic endeavor, but it is more—a call to the confident hope enshrined in the heart of the gospel: "Heaven and earth will pass away, but my words will not pass away" (Mark 13:31).

When the Kirchentag of 1954 was held behind the Iron Curtain at Leipzig the scores of thousands of embattled Christians who attended centered their study and worship around the theme, "Rejoicing in Hope." Dramatically symbolic was a climactic youth rally in the city's largest convention hall, at which twenty thousand young Christians from both the East and the West worshiped in a room whose permanent decorations featured the skyline of Moscow etched on glass that spanned one giant wall. This representation of the Mecca of a materialist order seemed destined to dominate the gathering. But towering before it soared a heroic cross; and as the meeting closed, the roll of the churches called delegation after delegation into what seemed a world-girdling circle with the cross at its center. In that unity of East and West around the cross, empowered by a faith which kept them—despite tyrannous repressions—"rejoicing in hope," the young people who lived at the heart of crisis made their answer. It is an answer that can give power to the preaching the contemporary mind desperately needs to hear: Events have not outrun God's competence and control; living by that faith we can join with him in making crisis redemptive and creative.

For Further Study

1. The preacher cannot hope to master the technicalities involved in questions of armaments and their control, yet he ought not to speak of these matters without some intelligent grasp of the nature of the problems they entail. For background information on the development of nuclear arms, a basic source is Arthur Holly Compton, *Atomic Quest* (New York: Oxford University Press, 1956). Concerning the human implications of nuclear weapons Linus Pauling, *No More War* (New York: Dodd, Mead and Company, 1958) brings together the relevant data from both the physical and biological sciences. Nobel Prize chemist Pauling interprets the work of top level scientists in these various fields authoritatively but with remarkable skill in making them understandable to the layman. An ethical and religious evaluation of these problems from a variety of informed viewpoints is made compactly available in *God and the H-Bomb*, edited by Donald Keyes (New York: Bellmeadows Press and Bernard Geiss Associates, 1961) and in a booklet symposium edited by William Clancy, *The Moral Dilemma of Nuclear Weapons* (New York: The Church Peace Union, 1961). On problems of arms control and disarmament the most authoritative source of information is the symposium of scientists and strategic experts edited by Donald G. Brennan, *Arms Control, Disarmament, and National Security* (New York: George Braziller, 1961) published under sponsorship of the American Academy of Arts and Sciences. Two books, briefer and less technical, but informed and of divergent viewpoints are: Richard J. Barnet, *Who Wants Disarmament?* (Boston: The Beacon Press, 1960); and Arthur T. Hadley, *The Nation's Safety and Arms Control* (New York: The Viking Press, 1961). An eloquent plea for the venture toward world order under a strengthened United Nations is offered by Norman Cousins, *In Place of Folly* (New York: Harper and Row, 1961).

2. Books on race relations are numerous. A small library useful to the preacher might include: Ethel J. Alpenfels, *Sense and Nonsense*

About Race (New York: Friendship Press, 1957); Harriet Harmon Dexter, *What's Right with Race Relations* (New York: Harper and Row, 1958); Benjamin E. Mays, *Seeking to Be Christian in Race Relations* (New York: Friendship Press, 1957); Liston Pope, *Kingdom Beyond Caste* (New York: Friendship Press, 1957).

3. The Christian concerns considered in this chapter have an urgency which defies relegation to special days in the church calendar. Yet the topical interests of certain days bring them into the foreground of normal attention for preachers and congregation alike. Some denominations observe a Race Relations Day in February; for those which do not, Brotherhood Day (the Sunday nearest February 22) is a general community observance of great importance to Christians. World Order Sunday (nearest Sunday to October 24, birthday of the United Nations) and World Peace Sunday (nearest Sunday to November 11) afford opportunities to stress the religious viewpoint on matters of importance to the general community.

From the vistas of thought and investigation suggested in this chapter, select a subject for one of these special days, make your double analysis of a scripture text, formulate a proposition, and develop a sermon. Remember, as you do so, that one cannot say anything worth saying in these areas without involving himself in what will be controversial for some part of his congregation. Consequently it will be important to bear in mind the principles for preaching on controversial issues (see pages 75-80) as you work out this sermon.

4. Special days do not exhaust the significance of these concerns. Note how they relate themselves to many aspects of the church year, on which we can here offer only a few suggestive comments:

a) Advent, which is far more than a foreshadowing of Christmas, sounds the note of "the God who comes"—God as sovereign Judge of history. This chapter has noted the relation of that theme to these urgent contemporary issues (pages 146-148).

b) Epiphany and the season it controls are devoted to the revelation of Christ to the Gentiles, and to the unveiling of the light of the knowledge of God in the face of Jesus Christ to widening circles of world concern. Any realistic grappling with this message must inevitably come, somewhere in the course of the Epiphany season, to a forthright confrontation between Christ and the crisis of our time (pages 148-150).

c) Lent's probing of moral issues, and its focus on the Cross, lead, somewhere in their development, to issues as vital to our destiny as these which we have been considering, and to an encounter with convictions which involve purposeful cross-bearing in our age.

d) Easter's triumphant note should not be dissipated in a single festival Sunday. The full season of Eastertide is needed for its message —a season more than ever important in an age living under the shadow of universal death. The season speaks to the personal aspects of crisis, with assurance of God's gift of triumph over death. It speaks, too, of God's answer to the crosses erected by man's pride and power. Surely there is a message here concerning the massive evils which erect such crosses now.

e) Pentecost and the Sundays which follow it celebrate the coming of the Holy Spirit to call forth a people of God, a new Israel. Pages 150-51 suggest a relationship between this theme and the contemporary crisis, which will warrant greatly extended investigation.

f) The Christian calendar instituted by the Federal Council of Churches and continued by the National Council, closes the church year with the season of Kingdomtide, extending from the last Sunday in August (Festival of Christ the King) to the beginning of Advent. It is obvious that such an extended period devoted to considerations centering in our Lord's kingship and the nature of his kingdom could only with great difficulty ignore its implications concerning the creative and redemptive facing of the major issues of this age of crisis.

It is not proposed that the pulpit exploit all these occasions for repeated sermons on crisis. Often the most effective preaching on such issues as this chapter indicates is not done in a full-scale assault running through a whole sermon, but in a strong section of a sermon other parts of which look in less controversial directions. What we are suggesting is the way in which the church year invites such treatment again and again in relation to the variety of gospel themes it passes in review.

Why not begin now to explore a theme for the next season after the one in which you read this chapter, from which you will develop a sermon designed to help your people to live more confidently and creatively in this time of crisis?

appendix

a notebook dialogue
with contemporary axioms

By way of illustration, the following sketches are offered to indicate the significance of the challenged axiom in precipitating sermon starters which engage the contemporary mind in fruitful dialogue. No attempt has been made to indicate the development of the potential sermon to which each sketch is an invitation. All that is undertaken is the striking of a spark, as the flint and steel of Scripture and a contemporary axiom are brought sharply together. If the spark lodges in the mind of the reader to ignite a helpful sermon, an incidental purpose will be served. But the deeper intent of these pages is to incite encounters between other contemporary axioms discovered or distilled by the reader (as proposed in pages 71-75), and the Word.

The sermon starters experimentally offered here are based successively on the eleven "Axioms of the Modern Man" composed by Emil Brunner.[1]

1. Everything is relative.
2. What can't be proved can't be believed.
3. Scientific knowledge is certain and the standard of truth; matters of faith are uncertain.
4. Beyond death nobody knows.
5. "Real" means seen and handled.
6. The big things are the great things. Because man is so small in this big universe he is so little.
7. I cannot help being what I am.
8. Freedom means doing as I like.
9. Justice means equality.
10. To put religion first is religious arrogance.
11. Laws of nature determine everything.

Frontier of Relativity

Now if you are ready, as soon as you hear the sound of the horn, the pipe, the lyre, the trigon, the harp, the bagpipe, and every other kind of musical instrument, to fall down and prostrate your-selves before the image which I have made, well and good; but if you will not prostrate yourselves, you shall forthwith be cast into the midst of a furnace of flaming fire; and what god is there who shall deliver you out of my hands?

—Dan. 3:15 Amer. Trans.[2]

[1] *The Church's Witness to God's Design*, Vol. II of Man's Disorder and God's Design ("Amsterdam Assembly Series" [New York: Harper & Row, Publishers, 1949]), p. 81.

[2] *The Complete Bible: An American Translation*, trans. J. M. Powis Smith and Edgar J. Goodspeed. Copyright 1939 by the University of Chicago Press, p. 813.

So! Our everyday axiom, *"Everything is relative,"* is not so modern, after all! It is at least as old as Nebuchadnezzar. "Your God may have done very well for you among your own people. He had recognition there. But here what can he do for you? Bright young men like you must know that standards vary and gods have power according to the outlook of the people who surround you." So said Nebuchadnezzar. And so say modern relativists, playing latter-day variations on an ancient theme.

Relativity offers a helpful concept in the natural sciences. It does not follow that it tells the truth about the most distinctively human areas of experience or the final realities with which we must live. As a device in understanding others and making allowance for their failures, relativity has value. As a guide for conduct and belief it is bound to betray us. When the relativity principle is admitted, the door is opened to all the wish-fulfillments and rationalizings by which we deceive and undo ourselves.

One of John Steinbeck's characters muses on the proverb "Money has no heart," wondering if kindness would not be a weakness in a money man. "Morals are relative," he muses; and as for sin—"that's relative too in a relative universe." Recalling how patriotic and virtuous his ancestors seemed, founding the family fortune on their commissions to raid commerce in the Revolution and again in 1812, he adds: "But to the British they were pirates, and what they took they kept." [3] That train of thought launched him on a course which narrowly missed the depths of tragedy only because, at the eleventh hour, he was pulled back from a robbery he had carefully planned.

Concerned about this resurgent relativity, a metropolitan newspaper points up its implications: "Is an individual life more important than the life of a group?" it asks. "(The state, or the party, is more important than the people who compose it, say the totalitarians.) Where do you draw the line between

[3] Steinbeck, op. cit., p. 65.

voluntary co-operation and bowing to dictatorships? What's the difference between political control and business or social pressure?" [4]

To these disturbing questions Shadrach, Meschach, and Abednego returned an answer which still stands, pertinent and powerful. The Hebrew youths rejected the relativity which would adapt their behavior to their new surroundings, convinced that however the pressure of environment changed, they stood under a claim of conscience that allowed no compromise. To the king's decrees they replied. "If our God, whom we serve, is able to deliver us, he will deliver us out of the furnace of flaming fire, and out of your hand, O king; but if not, be it known to you, O king, we will not serve your gods, nor prostrate ourselves before the image of gold which you have set up." (Dan. 3:17-18, Amer. Trans.)

Note the crucial phrase: "But if not"! Even those who cannot be sure of ultimate absolutes in a metaphysical sense, can safeguard themselves and society only by loyalties to which they give absolute commitment. Here relativity reaches its last frontier.

Observing how we shrink from encounter with the crowd, Kierkegaard was certain that the pressure of majority mores is no safe guide. "Truth always rests with the minority," he declared, "and the minority is always stronger than the majority, because the minority is generally formed by those who really have an opinion." [5] The majority finally pays tribute to the few who know what they believe, by adopting their opinions however belatedly.

To accept "what's being done" as our guide is to forfeit what most makes for achievement. Even among animals the leaders scorn such relativity. A famous trainer of chimpanzees, asked how he put his troupe through their complex act under

[4] *Chicago Sun Times.*

[5] Søren Kierkegaard, *The Diary*, trans. Gerda M. Andersen, ed. Peter P. Rohde (New York: Philosophical Library, Inc., 1960), p. 106.

precise control, replied: "First, I stand back and watch a new group for a while to see who is going to be boss. Once that is settled I have little difficulty. The boss chimp, when I get him on my side, keeps the rest of them in line." [6] Even the "boss chimp" is not willing to settle for an easy-going shrug that says, "Everything is relative."

Leaders never are. Americans who value civil liberties have reason to be grateful to Mr. Gus Courts, of Humphreys County, Mississippi, who refused to believe that "Everything is relative" in the matter of voting rights. During the year 1955, pressure against the 400 registered voters among the county's 16,012 Negroes succeeded in removing all but one from the lists. But Gus Courts would not yield. A friend who held out with him was killed by a shotgun blast. The rent was tripled on the building in which Mr. Courts kept his grocery store. Wholesalers cut off his credit. After nearly a year of resistance, he too was shot, though he proved too stubborn to die. Not only for Negroes but for all Americans, civil liberties are made secure by the refusal of such men to accept the lie that custom is the arbiter of right.

A popular limerick aptly lampoons our timid notion that new times and new customs abrogate tested standards:

> There was a young girl from a Mission,
> Who was seized by a dreadful suspicion
>   That original sin
>   Didn't matter a pin
> In the era of nuclear fission.

What a far cry that, from Shadrack and his companions, facing a strange new time and its pagan customs with their defiant challenge: "We will not serve your gods"!

Dr. Albert Einstein, father of the relativity theory as ap-

* Vance Packard, *The Status Seekers* (New York: David McKay, Co., Inc., 1959), p. 18.

plied to the physical universe, emphatically repudiated it as applied to human conduct. A questioner asked him what would happen to human morals if intelligent life were found on other planets. "Is morality merely based on the accumulated experience of mankind and therefore limited to our earth?" the interviewer inquired. Thoughtfully Einstein replied, "The universe is fully consistent. It is a unity. The same physical laws that regulate the movements of our planet control also the most distant stars. . . . Likewise the moral law that governs us holds sway in the farthest reaches of the universe." [7]

Like Abraham of old, the great physicist knew that relativity stops at the frontier where tested loyalties meet the pressure of lower mores. As a distinguished rabbi observes, when the Bible speaks of Abraham at home, it says, "And Abraham dwelt." When he went abroad among people whose standards violated his own, the term changes; then it says: "And Abraham sojourned." Shadrack and his friends were true sons of Abraham. They could *sojourn* among the pagan Babylonians because they *dwelt* in a place of tested truth.

What about us?

Realities We Do Not See

Faith gives substance to our hopes, and makes us certain of realities we do not see.   —Heb. 11:1 N.E.B.

How oddly that compares with the creeping prudentialism of the modern mind as it clings to its maxim, "*What can't be proved can't be believed.*" Christians cannot pretend to offer proof, but the world would be poorer without their mighty belief. "Certain of realities we do not see"—it is no accident that these words introduce the roster of a nation's heroes which occupies the rest of the chapter. What a

[7] John Sutherland Bonnell, *Certainties for Uncertain Times* (New York: Harper & Row, Publishers, 1962), p. 130.

whittled-down history Israel would have inherited, had these adventurers confined themselves to this dull positivism that "What can't be proved can't be believed."

Proof is not all of one sort. There is proof by logical demonstration, proof by controlled experiment, proof inferred from emperical evidence. In all meaningful personal relations we act where we cannot prove. Try friendship, love, patriotism, without commitment that outruns proof! The scientist can prove a scientific proposition; he cannot in the same sense prove that truth is *worth* the costly toil he devotes to its service. In his major commitment he acts by faith.

So—and from the same necessity—does religion.

> How is it proved?
> It isn't proved, you fool, it can't be proved.
> How can you prove a victory before
> It's won? How can you prove a man who leads,
> To be a leader worth the following,
> Unless you follow to the death? And out
> Beyond mere death, which is not anything
> But Satan's lie upon eternal life.
> Well—God's my leader, and I hold that He
> Is good, and strong enough to work His plan
> And purpose out to its appointed end.[8]

Limit belief to logically proved propositions if you must—and if you are prepared to sacrifice all high personal relations, cut the nerve of achievement, and rob the world of heroes!

One hero you would lose was Vernon Johns, who helped prepare the way for the achievements of Martin Luther King. A decade before King became its pastor, Vernon Johns shepherded the the congregation of Dexter Avenue Baptist Church in Montgomery, Alabama. On one occasion he posted this sermon subject on the church's bulletin board: "Policemen

[8] "Faith," by G. A. Studdert-Kennedy. From: *The Sorrows of God and Other Poems.* Copyright by Harper & Row, Publishers, Inc., P. 15.

Can Kill a Negro Boy in Montgomery, Alabama." Because it referred to a fresh incident of police violence, the sermon was delivered to an interracial congregation that packed the church. Johns never finished the message. Midway in its delivery, he was interrupted by policemen who arrested him in his pulpit; but the unfinished sermon had a power that still goes on. As a Negro college president observed, "Men like King don't just happen. They're the result of little known but powerful forces behind them. In Montgomery that force began with the Rev. Vernon Johns." [9] His faith, venturing in the name of "realities we do not see," found vindication.

Sometimes this faith impels such forthright witness; but it calls again for the reverent silence before a fellow-human without which there is no real understanding. Ignazio Silone has compared us to a colony of refugees who, from morning to night, "spend most of their time telling one another the story of their lives. The stories are anything but amusing, but they tell them to one another, really, in an effort to make themselves understood." [10] In our clatter of voices nothing is so much needed as the capacity to be quiet before "realities we do not see" hidden deep within a fellow-mortal. So, in his *Letters and Papers from Prison*, the heroic Dietrich Bonhoeffer called us to "fight for a revival of a wholesome reserve between man and man"—the preservation of an area of privacy and mystery which we refuse to invade, entering only on invitation. Only so can we deal with what Silone called "the inmost reality of people."

If faith powers the witness that opens the way to some realities and hushes us into silence that discovers others, it also commands a modesty about our explanations of things, which is essential to true knowledge. Watching an able physicist, Kierkegaard remarked on how this "gifted man is

[9] Harriet Harmon Dexter, *What's Right with Race Relations* (New York: Harper & Row, Publishers, 1958), pp. 227-28.

[10] Quoted in William Hamilton, *The New Essence of Christianity* (New York: Association Press, 1961), p. 25.

able to explain Nature, but does not understand his own self." For, said Kierkegaard, like most of us, he was busily trying to explain his own reality by reducing it to some simple "X." "But when everything is explained through an 'X' which is not explained, then *in toto* nothing is explained, nothing at all." [11]

Faith has long known that secret; for, beyond proof, it "makes us certain of realities we do not see," and without which we cannot live.

Adventure in Certainty

I know whom I have believed and I am sure that he is able to guard until that Day what has been entrusted to me.

—II Tim. 1:12

"I am sure!" How? Not by reading the answer in the back of the book! Not by betting on a sure thing! Not by having a proven guarantee before he took the first step.

Pathetic, isn't it? to be confined to an unproved surmise. Who knows but it is mere wish-fulfillment? What can you do with such frail stuff? Very little—except be involved in life's grandest adventures, give yourself away to One who puts life's broken pieces together in the most meaningful pattern, and build a new age on the crumbling ruins of a rotting paganism. To such adventures this pathetic certainty led.

We, of course, are wiser. We know a way to make sure in advance, or so we say: "*Scientific knowledge is certain and the standard of truth; matters of faith are uncertain.*" But it's worth noting that scientific knowledge is not "certain" in quite the way popular belief assumes. It was *scientists* who first resisted the Darwinian concepts and the work of Pasteur—in the name of their science. Scientific theories change from generation to generation: one system of astronomy succeeds another; geometry is Euclidian or non-Euclidian; the atom gives

[11] *Op. cit.*, pp. 98 f.

way to the electron as the ultimate unit; scientists come to look on their findings as "pointer readings."

In science, as in religion, what remains constant is exactly a "matter of faith." That natural phenomena have a dependable uniformity of behavior; that man's investigative reason can discover truth; that scientific method and inductive processes can lead to real knowledge and control; that truth itself is worth all its pursuit may cost—these unprovable assumptions are the foundation of science. As in the field of religion, experience tends to bear them out, but initially every one of them is a matter of faith.

When matters of faith move into the realm of personal relations that have met life's tests, they become certitudes on which to build with confidence. James Thurber has spoken some needed sanity about such foundations, in his protest against our folk-superstition that "love" between two undisciplined and immature people "is a push button solution, or instant cure for discontent." Declaring that "by our sentimental ignorance we encourage marriage as a kind of tranquilizing drug," he goes on to a memorable definition of the only love that has any stuff of stability. "A lady of 47 who has been married 27 years and has 6 children knows what love really is and once described it for me like this: 'Love is what you've been through with somebody.' " [12] On similar grounds the apostle declared, "I know whom I have believed." Leagues removed from that is this dilettante declaration that "Scientific knowledge is certain and the standard of truth," while "matters of faith are uncertain."

The distinguished psychoanalyst, Erich Fromm, observes that this demand for infallible proof is the mark of the paranoid. Faith in what reasonably *could* be, he says, must take the place of demands for what is *proven* beyond doubt, if humanity is to escape a nuclear Armageddon. "In the current discussion on armament control," he writes,

[12] As quoted in Robert Warren Spike, *To Be a Man* (New York: Association Press, 1961), pp. 71-72.

many arguments are based on the question of what is *possible*, rather than what is *probable*. The difference between these two modes of thinking is precisely the difference between *paranoid* and *sane* thinking. The paranoiac's unshakable conviction in the validity of his delusion rests upon the fact that it is logically possible, and, so, unassailable.[13]

You may show him that it is not at all probable that his family or associates are plotting against him; but, short of unassailable proof that it is not possible that they *might*, he knows no peace. Unless some healthy faith to venture on the probable replaces our cowering fear of *possible* threats and dangers, Fromm asserts, we have no foundation on which to build a stable world.

This venturing faith is forever withheld from the timorous for whom knowledge of the end must precede the first step of the journey. Dr. Carl Goerdeler, one of the heroes of the resistance movement within Hitler's Germany, proved that faith in the crucible of his suffering at the hands of the Gestapo. At his life's end he questioned the settled formulas of religion. Was there a God? If so, he had "permitted a few hundred thousand men bestialized, insane or blinded to drown mankind in rivers of blood and agony." But faith outlived crumbling formulas, sustaining a heroism which cried at the end, "Still I seek through Christ this merciful God. I have not found him. O Christ, where lies the truth, where is the consolation?" [14] God might be unseen, his ways beyond understanding, but Christ stood as the fixed point on his life's map.

So said the apostle, "I know whom I have believed and am sure that he is able to guard until that Day what has been entrusted to me." No scientific knowledge that! But it pro-

[13] Brennan, *op. cit.*, p. 195.

[14] As quoted in William Hamilton, *op. cit.*, p. 48, from Gehard Ritter, *The German Resistance* (New York: Frederick A. Praeger, 1958), p. 311.

vided a base for history's boldest, most productive venture. And the centuries have stood by it.

Robbing Death of Absurdity

If in this life we who are in Christ have only hope, we are of all men most to be pitied.

—I Cor. 15:19

Contemporary axioms assume that hope is all we have, and a dim hope at that. *"Beyond death nobody knows,"* we say. The presumption is that, of course, no sane man would give a moment's credence to a surmise as dim as *that.*

"True!" replies the Christian, nothing daunted. "Beyond death nobody does know. We neither claim nor want blueprints of heaven or chemical reports on hell. Pearly gates, streets of gold, and a lake of fire give us bold, vivid figures, symbols to aid our thinking about what admittedly 'eye hath not seen, nor ear heard.' We can speak of eternity only in the language of time. He is wise who understands that our words are but pointers to a single truth: God's love will hold us through eternity in a life rich and secure. In such knowledge as rests on sight, logic, or experiment, we gladly agree that 'beyond death nobody knows.' Who ever supposed anybody could?"

By the same token, no knowledge can deny the resurrection. Faith has its own valid grounds for believing that life triumphs over death. Families of ideas, important in themselves, vindicated by a world of experience, require this faith for their completion. They stand up to life. They are consistent with much else that we know. But you cannot make sense of them unless Christendom's resurrection faith is true.

If death has the last word, materialists pronounce doom on everything; but if beyond death lies reality, spirit triumphs. For those who believe in the God and Father of our Lord Jesus Christ, resurrection and the life everlasting make the best sense of our experience. Explore this family of ideas with

170

Paul in I Cor. 15:12-19, and see how three powerful truths twine themselves around the resurrection.

First, that to delete resurrection from faith's horizon you must begin by erasing it from history: "If there is no resurrection of the dead, then Christ has not been raised." But Christian faith won its way against persecutions and impossible odds as a faith in a Lord who died and rose again. To erase the resurrection from history you must take away the faith of 900,-000,000 people—a third of the earth's population. You must pull down the crosses—symbols of no dead, martyred Jesus but of a Christ who conquered death—from the spires that crown ten thousand hills. You must destroy many of the choicest canvases in the art galleries of the world. You must expunge a key word not only from Christian writings, but from such passages in the Koran as its promise: "Wherever ye be, God will bring you all back at the resurrection." You must draw the censor's pencil not through the writings of theologians only, but those of even such secular philosophers as Schopenhauer, as he declares that "Every parting gives a foretaste of death; every coming together again a foretaste of the resurrection." This is the first truth: resurrection is so plowed into history that if you remove it you leave the face of civilization an unrecognizable ruin.

And there is a second: that to delete the resurrection you must excise it from experience. In Paul's words, "If Christ has not been raised, your faith is futile and you are still in your sins." But millions have found, through him, a life so real and so new that to deny his liberating power would be to them the arch-absurdity. Albert Schweitzer spoke for these when he declared that the transforming power comes from a Christ who is not a historical memory but a living presence: "Not the historical Jesus, but the spirit that goes forth from Him and in the spirits of men strives for new influence and rule, is that which overcomes the world." [15] To get rid of the res-

---

[15] Charles R. Joy (ed.), *Albert Schweitzer; An Anthology* (New York: Harper & Row, Publishers, 1947), p. 82.

urrection you must cancel that experience; so runs the second truth in our family of ideas.

See, then, the third: that to delete the resurrection you must begin over again in all your thinking about God. "We are found to be misrepresenting God," wrote Paul, "because we testified of God that he raised Christ, whom he did not raise if it is true that the dead are not raised." If, when a boy is felled by a bullet, he falls never to rise again, the boy and the bullet are of the same order of reality and come to the same end. But if that is true, all that the best of men have believed about God's love for his children, and about an order of value above the material, must come to naught. Belief in God's love which gives the lie to death, sustains the achievements of men. A sociologist, talking about the ambitions that drive our higher efforts, remarked that "only when one knows where his next month's food and shelter will come from can he and his children afford to go in for long term education and training." [16] In the same way, those who have dared the hardest adventures and the most frightful martyrdoms have done so in the security that nothing in all creation—not even death—could separate them from the love of God.

All this takes on a new urgency in our generation, threatened by extinction. As James R. Newman put it, "The proposition that we all have to die some day is not the same as that we all have to die the same day." [17] Yet that proposition is now seriously considered by distinguished nuclear scientists. In such an age there is a new poignancy in Paul's words, "If it is for this life only that Christ has given us hope, we are of all men most to be pitied." (N.E.B.)

Defying the Tyranny of the Tangible
In the beginning was the Word.
—John 1:1

Which is Christianity's way of indicating the reality to

---

[16] Allison Davis, as quoted in Vance Packard, op. cit., p. 43.
[17] *The Rule of Folly* (New York: Simon and Schuster, Inc., 1962), p. 35.

which all else owes its existence. And that runs into a head-on collision with the mind of our age, which sets it down as axiomatic that " 'Real' means seen and handled."

Just how "real" are such things? Sir Osbert Sitwell, after a fascinating lifetime among those who had more than their share of the seen and handled, wrote sadly of its transciency. See his vivid picture of one of his friends in the 1920's:

Except for getting up in the late afternoon to take a single photograph for an immense fee, he stayed in bed all day, telephoning to Wall Street to buy shares on margin, and invariably got up in the evening in time for dinner—at which he always ate oyster-crabs Newburg, a specialty of New York—a much richer man on paper than when he had gone to bed the night before. Alas, this state of affairs was drawing to a close, but nobody knew it. People presumed that it would last forever.[18]

Presumed, that is, that things seen and handled are assuredly "real."

Contrast that paltry "reality" with the art collector Sir Osbert recalls "who had gone blind and whose chief pleasure it was to take people round his pictures, pointing out to them the particular beauties and subtleties of color and detail. So well had he known them, so much had he loved them while he still retained his sight that he never made a mistake." [19] He lived with realities of beauty which his seeing guests had never dimly glimpsed.

What about this bland assumption that " 'Real' means seen and handled"? Can you trust it? Not if the "real" is the durable! You can burn books; you cannot burn an idea. Blast a bridge, and the concept "to bridge" will fling another span across the channel. Things seen and handled pass; things believed and deeply felt remain.

Nor are things seen and handled the real causes of events.

[18] "New York in the Twenties" *The Atlantic*, Vol. LLIX, No. 2. (February, 1962), p. 38. Used by permission of Sir Osbert Sitwell.
[19] *Ibid.*, pp. 42-43.

Purposes are far more causal. Is an assembly line, with all its automated machines, the cause of an automobile? Must you not look deeper, in the region of the personal purposes of manufacturers and the buying public? Let the machines collide with some new idea which better fulfills the wants and purposes of persons, and then ask which is the more real.

So, in a sense more cosmic, says the gospel. "In the beginning was the Word, and the Word was with God, and the Word was God. . . . All things were made through him, and without him was not anything made that was made." (John 1:1, 3.)

You have not touched the fringe of reality until you have grasped that!

Pawns—or Heirs?

When I look at thy heavens, the work of thy fingers,
    the moon and the stars which thou hast established;
what is man?

—Ps. 8:3-4

Awed by the million-light-year bottomless depths of the universe, we can go this far with the psalmist. Indeed, what *is* man? *"The big things,"* we say, *"are the great things. Because man is so small in this big universe he is so little."* And yet . . .

Size cannot confer value. One small diamond is more precious than a mountainous slag pile. A man is puny beside a horse; but he buys the horse and controls it. A princely estate is immensely bigger than a baby; yet to the father-owner, the baby is what it is all for. In the universe man's mind achieves fragments of understanding and some limited areas of control; man's spirit is what it is for. Read with the psalmist beyond that fragmentary opening which sustains our timid skepticism.

When I look at thy heavens, the work of thy fingers,
    the moon and the stars, which thou hast established;

what is man that thou art mindful of him,
and the son of man that thou dost care for him?

Yet thou hast made him little less than God,
and dost crown him with glory and honor.
Thou hast given him dominion over the work of
thy hands.

—Ps. 8:3-6

That makes man great! What makes him "so little"? Forgetting on what his greatness rests, and presuming to stand on his own puny feet!

High-level military planners, standing thus, take upon themselves godlike decisions about the destinies of their neighbors and of generations yet unborn. Thus Herman Kahn speculates that "it might well turn out, for example, that U. S. decision makers would be willing, among other things, to accept the high risk of an additional 1 per cent of our children being born deformed *if that meant not giving up Europe to Soviet Russia.*" [20] Have such decision makers ever shared the grief of even a single home into which a child was born handicapped by deformity? Have they looked with awakened imagination into the life-long privations and bitter heartaches of such a child? And are they indeed willing to "accept" the prospect of more than 42,000 such deformed births every year —which is what their "additional 1 per cent of our children" would mean at the present birth rate? But this is only the beginning of the cost Mr. Kahn is talking about, for he anticipates the making of such payment by "twenty or thirty or forty generations" following a nuclear war. To such a pyramiding of woe do we commit ourselves when we presume to stand in our own right and make decisions reserved for God alone.

When we lose the conviction that every man is God's child, made "a little less than God," substituting for it our

---

[20] As quoted in James R. Newman, *op. cit.*, p. 21.

pathetic depreciation of a human life as "so small in this big universe," we replace persons with paper, souls with systems. Witness the observations reported by Martha Gellhorn at the trial of Adolf Eichmann for the murder of six million Jews. She describes the impassive unconcern with which he listens to the stories of tortured men and women. Only when documents are presented, she says, does he brighten to alertness, "when he can shift the piles of folders on his desk, sort, search for a paper, make notes: the organization man at his chosen task." [21]

In Adolf Eichmann it all comes to dramatic focus, but the human insensitivity reached much farther. There was a world-wide sin of indifference which, offering no asylum to the persecuted Jews, condemned them to their frightful fate in a Germany from which they could not escape. We might have offered them haven but we did not. "The inexorable consequence of this failure to seize a frantically urgent moral opportunity," wrote Rabbi David Polish, "has plunged much of contemporary Christianity into morbid preoccupation with esoteric doctrines which reject society and turn pathetically to a remote and forbidding God." [22]

"Thou hast made him little less than God"—knowing that makes man great and holds God close. When we forget that, man is dwarfed in an overpowering universe and God is lost in "esoteric doctrines."

Circumstance—and the Grace of God

But by the grace of God I am what I am.
—I Cor. 15:10

Popular notions dismiss that as naïve, even silly, substituting a proverbial fatalism which says: *"I cannot help being what I am."*

Can't you? "Here I stand; I cannot do otherwise. God

---

[21] *The Atlantic*, op. cit., p. 52. Used by permission of Martha Gellhorn.
[22] David Polish, *The Eternal Dissent* (New York: Abelard-Schuman Limited, 1960), p. 173.

help me"—once a man said that in defiance of the world. Do you now propose to say it in abject surrender?

With a little psychological sophistication, what imposing ways we can find to rationalize our excuse that we can't help being what we are: We were given a bad start by overprotective parents. Our environment dragged us down. Our weaknesses were built in by our biological inheritance. We have become the victims of drives and compulsions we were powerless to control. So the case runs on to its impressive total of personal helplessness. One question, however, raised by a minister whose psychological skill as a counselor is known across the nation, we dare not overlook: "Does it never occur to us that calling a thing by a big psychological name does not make it any better, and does not necessarily absolve us?" [23]

Heredity and environment create conditions we must cope with. They define problems. They give nudges in their own asburd directions. Conditioning factors forecast statistical probabilities: put x number of men in y circumstances, and for a predictable per cent of them z will follow. But individuals defy averages. Persons choose. Out of the ignorance and bigotry of New Salem, Lincoln rises. From an East Side slum comes Jacob Riis. And once it was asked, "Can anything good come out of Nazareth?" (John 1:46.)

Two replies to circumstance are possible, not one. You can say, "I cannot help being what I am." Or you can reply with the most defiant word in any language: "But!" "But by the grace of God I am what I am." No pattern of circumstance can predict the end of the journey which begins there.

Wearing Freedom's Yoke

If you continue in my word, you are truly my disciples, and you will know the truth, and the truth will make you free.

—John 8:31-32

Is that freedom? "Continue in my word?" Begin there

[23] Bonnell, op. cit., p. 145.

and you have already given away the chance to do as you please, which is to say you have renounced freedom. For, according to popular definition, "*Freedom means doing as I like.*"

Perhaps. But freedom of undisciplined impulse operates in a steadily shrinking field. Jacques Maritain declared that no more penetrating question can be asked about a man than whether he regards freedom as primarily a throwing off or a taking on of limitations. Try that out in any realm—finance, athletics, domestic happiness, the arts. Freedom means attaining, through discipline, the capacity to achieve in ever wider areas, to expand the range in which effective choices can be made.

One who had paid the price to know said the true word about freedom: "The gate is narrow and the way is hard, that leads to life, and those who find it are few" (Matt. 7:14). That, as any man with half an eye can see, is the exact opposite of "doing as I like." It is also one of the mightiest defenses against fear, a chief foe of do-as-you-like freedom. If following impulse is the chief mark of the free man, he must live in constant fear of the impulses of others who practice his kind of freedom. They hazard his life on highways where doing as they like means drinking before they drive. They increase his tax load by following the impulse to chisel their own tax return. They endanger the peace of a predominantly non-white world by indulging their prejudices against people of color. In the wake of their adventures in undisciplined living, fears multiply.

And fear destroys freedom. Fear prompted us to wartime betrayal of our own principles of freedom by herding behind barbed wire some 75,000 American citizens whose parents had come from Japan—against not one of whom any charge of disloyalty had been made, much less proved. Fear supplied the motive for taking qualities which we saw in ourselves and others as virtues, and turning them into threats when we saw them in these people of oriental background. What had we against them? "They were industrious, skillful, intelligent, ambitious; and instead of being willing to live in ghettos, they wanted homes in good parts of the cities. They incorporated too many traits that made people successful, and thus became a threat to Americans." [24]

General Eisenhower has spoken of fears that endanger our freedom in this period of "cold war." In our timorousness, he says, we picture our enemies as "eight feet tall." Those who are influenced by the John Birch Society and similar movements of the radical right grow so fearful of the weaknesses of democracy that they accuse great numbers of our elected officials of being "soft on communism" or subverted by its intrigues. Fear feeds on fear to produce a people sick with suspicion of their neighbors, ripe for the picking by demagogues who, like Hitler, destroy freedom on the pretext of defending it.

Yet there is another way, better and more durable. But it is open only to the courageous who have learned to practice inner discipline founded on a mighty faith: "If you continue in my word, you are truly my disciples, and you will know the truth, and the truth will make you free."

The "word" in which the Pioneer of that freedom called us to continue included his counsel in a story about those who asked, "Lord, when was it that we saw you hungry or thirsty or a stranger or naked or ill or in prison, and did nothing for you?" The answer they received was plain: "I tell you this: anything you did not do for one of these, however humble, you did not do for me" (Matt. 25:44-45 N.E.B.). Some advice once given by Henry Ford fits the bent of our minds more comfortably, however. "I do not believe that a man can ever leave his business," he said. "He ought to think of it by day and dream of it by night. . . . Thinking men know that work is the salvation of the race, morally, physically, socially. Work does more than get us a living; it gets us a life."

[24] Dexter, op. cit., p. 27.

Halford Luccock has reminded us that such advice is safe to live with only when we see our business in the wider terms reported at long last by the ghost of Jacob Marley, of Dickens' *Christmas Carol* fame: "Business! . . . Mankind was my business. The common welfare was my business; charity, mercy, forbearance, and benevolence were my business. The dealings of my trade were but a drop of water in the comprehensive ocean of my business." [25]

Amid such business, fear flees and freedom flourishes.

When Justice Learns From Grace

Lo, these many years I have served you, and I never disobeyed your command; yet you never gave me a kid, that I might make merry with my friends. But when this son of yours came, who has devoured your living with harlots, you killed for him the fatted calf!
—Luke 15:29-30

Anyone can see that the son who said this had grounds for grievance. In our brief everyday definitions, "*Justice means equality.*" By that formula, scant justice had been done him.

In one sense it is profoundly true that "justice means equality,"—in equal rights before the law that principle is indispensable. May it ever be cherished by free men.

When they deny it, exorbitant costs accrue. Mississippi, regarding itself the most peaceful state because the most segregated, found in 1958—before Hawaii and Alaska gained statehood—that it ranked forty-eighth in industrial growth. Its Negroes were moving away, but so too were many of its white citizens; in eight years twenty counties lost a sixth of their white population, one lost a half. The governor's struggle to bring new industry to the state proved futile in the face of determined resistance to school desegregation and the right of Negroes to vote.[26] So costly was the price paid by a community for its denial that justice means equality.

[25] Halford E. Loccock, *More Preaching Values in the Epistles of Paul* (New York: Harper & Row, Publishers, 1961), p. 151.
[26] Dexter, *op. cit.*, p. 75.

Yet does equality fully define justice? What about the semi-skilled worker with a twenty-five-year record of faithful service, who discovers that the seventeen-year-old high school drop-out at the next machine is earning almost exactly what he is? Then some searching questions need to be asked about equality. Is it just to give equal pay despite such differences, or when needs and responsibilities are vastly unequal?

Are the ends of justice served best when every man lives jealously on guard in the attitude of vigilant assertion that "I'm as good as you are"? From a naturalistic point of view, all men are born unequal. Can an arbitrary leveling down of inequalities—flattening out differences in talent and its expression, for instance—produce a justice you can long keep or greatly care to have?

Only from a deeply religious point of view are all men created equal. All share equally in the Father's love, birthright of children in one family. Family equality does not pour all into one mold; it treasures the talents of the gifted, but lavishes special love on the handicapped. It is born of common loyalties, shared responsibilities, mutual affection, and a common participation in the community created by parental love. Family justice is not harsh, but therapeutic; not assertive, but responsible; not contentious, but loving.

Once an older brother tried to force his father's hand by appeal to the notion that "justice means equality." The father's reply is a glimpse into the heart of God: "Son, you are always with me, and all that is mine is yours. It was fitting to make merry and be glad, for this your brother was dead, and is alive; he was lost, and is found." (Luke 15:31-32.)

There is a way of preaching this forgiving grace which awakens sympathy with the older brother's complaint. After listening to such a sermon, Kierkegaard reflected in his *Diary* that one is prompted to say to himself: "Ah, I get you; I see what I must do; all I have to do is get a little lax, for I have already become too perfect." From the preaching that rushes to the pulpit with Luther's counsel to "sin boldly" half-digested to mean that God loves riotous living more than disciplined service, may the good Lord deliver us!

The hard-working older brothers who stay home and mind the chores are not always easy to live with, however. A world made up of them would be no custom-built Utopia. They might easily rub each other the wrong way at so many points that peaceful community life would be impossible. "The saint, or the aspiring saint," as David Polish sees him, "is usually running off into the wilderness with a contempt for the group, altogether unbecoming to sainthood. The paradox of the redeemed individual is that he is not amenable to socialization." [27] That overlooks a considerable company of saints who have poured out their lives for others in a selflessness that bound the community in fellowship, but it also describes the older brother. "Justice means equality"—that he understood; but grace which could restore community by forgiving the unworthy lay utterly beyond his ken.

Yet it is exactly the unworthy who must be forgiven. The returning prodigal was not a basically fine, sweet personality with a few minor mistakes to be corrected. He could not come saying. "You know that I have many 'faults' and 'imperfections,' but do not look at these, but to my personality as a 'whole,' to the inner 'core.'" He must say rather: "I, just as I am in the inner recesses of my personality, am unworthy to be called your son." [28]

But that too is the prayer the hard-working older brother, sulking outside in unbrotherly anger, needed to learn to pray. Until it learned from grace, his plea of justice was not good enough.

Paradox of Christ's Intolerance

But seek first his kingdom and his righteousness, and all these things shall be yours as well.   —Matt. 6:33

[27] Op. cit., p. 65.

[28] Gustaf Aulen, The Faith of the Christian Church (Philadelphia: The Muhlenberg Press, 1960), p. 264.

That, says our popular wisdom, is an intolerable claim. *"To put religion first is religious arrogance."*

Perhaps so. It makes bigots. It leads to clericalism, sordid secularism in the garb of divinity. It sets vast bonfires of books —a monumental evil, whether the torch is lighted by Hitler in the name of the Third Reich or by Savanarola in the name of the Church.

Jesus wanted no part in putting religion first. God first he did demand: "You shall love the Lord your God with all . . ." And this claim, he said, had an identical twin: "You shall love your neighbor as yourself." (Mark 12:30-31.) Try these on for size, and see how much arrogance you find in them.

Men may bolster their hatred of Jews on some pretext that religion comes first, but the plea falls into silence before this law of love for God and neighbor. In humility we must confess that the ghastliest of all purges of Jews occurred in our generation. What had we been putting first? As a reporter of the Eichmann trial declared, to turn away from the awful facts because they are nauseatingly unpleasant is as irresponsible as it would be to turn away from cancer because it kills in wanton cruelty. We need to know all about the factors that produce cancer, that we may ward off its lethal approach; and we need to know every sign in ourselves and in society that signals the coming of anti-Semitism or any other such foul pestilence. Religious arrogance must be made to give way to realistic love of God and our neighbor.

Or try this corollary: "Whoever cares for his own safety is lost; but if a man will let himself be lost for my sake and for the Gospel, that man is safe" (Mark 8:35, N.E.B.). To see this law of life put to the test, one has only to watch Jesus gamble away his safety by declining the support of the revolutionary Zealot party of his time. In her play, *The Man Born to Be King*, Dorothy Sayers has Captain Baruch dictate a letter which, while not strictly historical, serves to dramatize the forces that were at work when Jesus came to Jerusalem for his last Passover. Baruch warns Jesus that the priests are plotting a violent end for him, but declares that with popular support and the aid of Zealot men and arms he cannot only escape this fate but rise triumphantly to power. Then he states the clear alternative that lay back of Jesus' entry into Jerusalem:

> When a king comes in peace, he rides upon an ass; but when he goes to war, upon a horse. In the stable of Zimri, at the going-up into the City, is a war-horse saddled and ready. Set yourself upon him, and you shall ride into Jerusalem with a thousand spears behind you. But if you refuse, then take the ass's colt that is tied at the vineyard door, and Baruch will bide his time till a bolder Messiah comes.[29]

Jesus chose the ass, and renounced his own safety and aggrandizement. "A thousand spears" did not follow him, but millions of men and women in all generations look to him as Savior.

We are not called to put religion first; we are called to put Christ first. "Whoever does not bear his own cross and come after me," he said, "cannot be my disciple." (Luke 14:27.) Such obedience is at the opposite pole from arrogance. Far from lording it over others, it denies self. It does not make pretenses; it accepts discipline. It judges no one; it searches and humbles self.

There is nothing apologetic about this charge, "Seek first his kingdom and his righteousness, and all these things shall be yours as well." It does not offer timid advice which we can accept or not according to our judgment. It states a law of life, puts before us an ultimate which we disregard at our peril. Soft-spoken salesmen may plead with us to adopt their wares, whether Christianity or beauty soap, but the gospel will have none of this inoffensive pleading. Rather it demands: God first! Christ first! Self in check, disciplined into freedom, fulfilled by denial! *Absolute* that is, but *arrogant* never.

[29] As quoted in Donald T. Rowlingson, *Jesus the Religious Ultimate* (New York: The Macmillan Company, 1961), p. 105.

When Spirit Breaks Law's Chain

For the law of the Spirit of life in Christ Jesus has set me free
from the law of sin and death.   —Rom. 8:2

With another saying about law the modern man is far
more at home. It is his axiom that *"Laws of nature determine
everything."*

But laws of nature are not static absolutes. That idea died
with the passe notions of the nineteenth century. Scientists
are more inclined to speak now of statistical probabilities than
of absolute determiners. Natural law is no closed system, auto-
matic and undeviating. Seeking knowledge in order to exercise control, science knows that laws can be used, and men
are the users. So it is not the laws that control, finally, but
the men. In the end, purpose controls—purpose implemented
by knowledge.

Wise men ask a key question about "laws of nature":
Laws in whose hands? Paul was taking hold of the matter by
that strategic handle when he wrote, "For the law of the Spirit
of life in Christ Jesus has set me free from the law of sin and
death." The victorious live by the law of the Spirit. No longer
pushed around by inanimate forces, they know a secret that
brings nature under control. "The law of sin and death"—
what could smack more of nature than that resounding phrase?
But it could not bind Paul. Not that it had not tried! Where
in all literature can you match Paul's sentence summary of
natural obstacles?

Three times I have been shipwrecked; a night and a day I have
been adrift at sea; on frequent journeys, in danger from rivers, dan-
ger from robbers, danger from my own people, danger from Gentiles, danger in the city, danger in the wilderness, danger at sea,
danger from false brethren; in toil and hardship, through many a
sleepless night, in hunger and thirst, often without food, in cold
and exposure.   —II Cor. 11:25-27

If laws of nature determine everything, how do you move

from that pageant of privation to this victorious valedictory? "For I am sure that neither death, nor life, nor angels, nor principalities, nor things present, nor things to come, nor powers, nor height, nor depth, nor anything else in all creation, will be able to separate us from the love of God in Christ Jesus our Lord." (Rom. 8:38-39.)

Paul himself, having lived through it all, was sure there could be only one explanation: "The law of the Spirit of life in Christ Jesus has set me free from the law of sin and death." There the two laws confront each other in the sharp contrast characteristic of both Paul's time and our own. In 1907, among papyrus fragments of an ancient lost gospel, a descriptive passage was found which brings to dramatic focus this contrast between the laws men find in experience and bind upon themselves, and the "law of the Spirit of life in Christ Jesus." It narrates the challenge issued to Jesus by a Pharisee who accused him of defiling the temple by entering without proper ceremonial washing.

And the Saviour straightway stood still with his disciples and answered him, Art thou then being here in the temple clean? He saith unto him, I am clean, for I washed in the pool of David, and having descended by one staircase I ascended by another and put on white and clean garments, and then I came and looked upon these holy vessels. The Saviour answered and said unto him, Woe ye blind, who see not! Thou hast washed in these running waters wherein dogs and swine have been cast night and day, and thou hast cleansed and wiped the outside skin which also harlots and flute-girls anoint and wash and wipe for the lust of men, but within they are full of scorpions and all wickedness. But I and my disciples who thou sayest have not bathed have been dipped in the waters of eternal life which come from God.[30]

For two millenia men have lived by that inner cleansing power which they found in him—"the law of the Spirit of life in Christ Jesus"—and it has not let them down.

[30] Leslie Paul, Son of Man (New York: E. P. Dutton and Co., Inc., 1961), pp. 173-74. Used by permission of Hodder & Stoughton, Ltd.

How failing, on the other hand has been the external law. None have tried harder to govern themselves nobly by the "laws of nature" than did the ancient Stoics. Hear how one of them described the futile struggle. One Serenus is writing to Seneca:

I find myself not quite free, nor yet quite in bondage to the faults which I feared and hated. . . . It is a weakness of the mind that sways between the two, that will neither bravely turn to right nor to wrong. . . . I beg you, if you have any remedy to stay my fluctuation of mind, count me worthy to owe you peace. To put what I endure into a simile, it is not the tempest that troubles me, but sea-sickness.[31]

How like our confusion! John P. Marquand, whose writing holds the mirror to our life at its more sophisticated levels, tells the story of a man who placed great importance on "being sincere," and who confesses as the story unfolds that he sometimes has great difficulty in knowing *how* to be sincere. For when sincerity ceases to be a spontaneous expression of the inner self, and becomes a consciously practiced posture, it ceases to be a dependable guide. The "law of the Spirit of life" is no longer in it.

Wise counselors see our need to return to a self so whole that it can come to spontaneous expression. So Erich Fromm says of his purpose as an analyst, that "analytic therapy is essentially an attempt to help the patient to gain or regain his capacity for love. If this aim is not fulfilled, nothing but surface changes can be accomplished." [32] So said Jesus, making love the central imperative of our life: "You shall love . . ." How can we love by command? Through love's contagion. "We love, because he first loved us" (I John 4:19).

Or, in Paul's summation, "The law of the Spirit of life in Christ Jesus has set me free from the law of sin and death."

[31] William Barclay, *The Mind of Jesus* (New York: Harper & Row, Publishers, 1961), p. 118.
[32] As quoted by Spike, *op. cit.*, p. 115.

index of scripture references

index of names and subjects